Bill Edwards

Willie Carmile

STANDARD ENCYCLOPEDIA OF

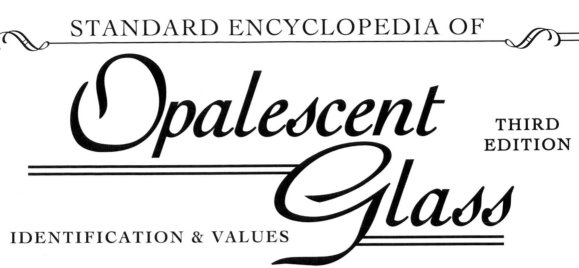

Opalescent Glass

THIRD EDITION

IDENTIFICATION & VALUES

Bill Edwards & Mike Carwile

COLLECTOR BOOKS
A Division of Schroeder Publishing Co., Inc.

The current values of this book should be used only as a guide. They are not intended to set prices, which vary from one section of the country to another. Auction prices as well as dealer prices vary and are affected by condition as well as demand. Neither the authors nor the publisher assumes responsibility for any losses that might be incurred as a result of consulting this guide.

Searching for a Publisher?

We are always looking for knowledgeable people considered to be experts within their fields. If you feel that there is a real need for a book on your collectible subject and have a large comprehensive collection, contact Collector Books.

On the Cover:

Cyclone Vase, Vaseline Opalescent, $800.00;
Kittens Cup and Saucer, Amethyst Opalescent, $1,000.00 (set);
Arabian Nights Pitcher, Cranberry Opalescent, $1,200.00.

Cover design by Beth Summers
Book design by Mary Ann Dorris

Contents

Part I

Opalescent Glass

1880 – 1930

Page 8

Part II

Whimsey Pieces

Page 154

Part III

Opalescent Glass

after 1930

Pago 178

Dedication

For Frank M. Fenton for his years of friendship and dedication.

Acknowledgments

Again, we gratefully acknowledge the aid of those who shared photos and information for this book with us. We depend on their help with each and every book and without their help, there just wouldn't be a book. Our thanks to Bonnie and Rick Boldt, Gene Serbus, Richard and Merri Houghton, Eugene Reno, Ray Jackson, Donna Drohan, Adam Fikso, Dave Peterson, Mary and Tom Greene, Janeane Schmidt, Steve and Radka Sandeman, John R. Loggie, III, Chris and Linda Kantzler, John E. Wray, John Coppenbarger, Jack Beckwith, Kathryn McIntyre, Richard Petersen, and anyone else we've overlooked.

Author's Note

In this third edition, I'd like to take the opportunity to introduce my new co-author and explain his coming aboard. His name is Mike Carwile and he lives with his family in Lynchburg, Virginia. He is very knowledgeable about all types of glass and brings to our work many years of glass experience.

The reason for this change is twofold: first, we are now doing three major glass books that are completely revised semi-annually, and the research has grown beyond any one person. And second, I've been writing books on glass for 27 years and I've reached the time in life when I want someone trained to carry on this task when I no longer can. Mike is just such a person.

I hope collectors will welcome this change that can only result in improved books down the road. Our sole purpose is to provide the best reference books possible for collectors.

Bill Edwards

Mike Carwile

Introduction

From its inception in the 1880s, opalescent glass has enjoyed a widely receptive audience, both in England where it was introduced and here in America where a young but growing market was ready for any touch of brightness and beauty for the hearth and home.

Early American makers, such as Hobbs, Brockunier and Company (1863 – 1888), Buckeye Glass (1878 – 1896), LaBelle Glass (1872 – 1888), American Glass (1889 – 1891), Nickel Plate Glass (1888 – 1893), and of course, the Northwood Glass Company in its various locations (1888 until its demise in 1924) were the primary producers, especially in early blown opalescent glass production. They were not by themselves, of course. Other companies such as Model Flint (1893 – 1899), Fostoria Shade & Lamp Co. (1890 – 1894), Consolidated Lamp & Glass (1894 – 1897), Elson Glass (1882 – 1893), West Virginia Glass (1893 – 1896), National Glass (1899 – 1903), Beaumont Glass (1895 – 1906), Dugan Glass (1904 – 1913) which then became Diamond Glass (1914 – 1931), and finally the Jefferson Glass Company (1900 – 1933) added their talents in all sorts of opalescent items in both blown and pressed glass.

The major production covered 40 years (1880 – 1920); however beginning shortly after the turn of the century, the Fenton Glass Company of Williamstown, West Virginia, joined the ranks of opalescent manufacturers and has continued production off and on until the present time. Their production from 1907 to 1940 is an important part of the opalescent field and has been covered to some extent in this book. The Fenton factory, along with Dugan and Jefferson glass, produced quality opalescent glass items long after the rest of the companies had ceased operations, primarily in pressed items in patterns they had used for other types of glassware.

In 1899 A. H. Heisey & Company began *very* limited production of some opalescent glass in white and blue by adding a milky formula to the glass while it was still in the mould. Patterns known are #1225 Pineapple and Fan in white and vaseline; #2 Plaid Chrysanthemum in vaseline (1904); #1220 Punty Band in white and blue (1904 – 1910); #1280 Winged Scroll in white (1910); #357 Prison Stripe in white (1905); #300 Peerless in blue; and a Pluto candlestick in experimental gold opalescent. Most of these were made in very small amounts for very short periods of time and by 1915 they were no longer in production.

To understand just what opalescent glass is has always been easy; to explain the process of making this glass is quite another matter. If the novice will think of two layers of glass, one colored and one clear, that have been fused so that the clear areas become milky when fired a second or third time, the picture of the process becomes easier to see. It is, of course, much more complicated than that, but for the sake of clarity, imagine the clear layer being pressed so that the second firing gives this opal milkyness to the outer edges, be they design or the edges themselves, and the process becomes clearer. It is, of course, the skill of the glassmaker to control this opalescence so that it does what he wants. It is a fascinating process and anyone who has had the privilege of watching a glassmaker at work can testify to it being a near-miracle.

Today, thousands of collectors seek opalescent glass and each has his or her own favorites. Current markets place blown opalescent glass as more desirable, with cranberry leading the color field, but there are many ways to collect, and groupings of one shape or one pattern or even one manufacturer are not uncommon. When you purchase this glass, the same rules apply as for any other glass collectible: (1) look for any damage and do not pay normal prices for damage; (2) choose good color as well as good milky opalescence; (3) **buy what pleases you!** You have to live with it, so buy what you like. To care for your glass, wash it carefully in lukewarm water and a mild soap; **never put old glass in a dishwasher!** Display your glass in an area that is well lighted and enjoy it!

Who Made It?

Confusion abounds over the Northwood/National/Dugan connection, as well as the Jefferson/Northwood connection. In 1896 Harry Northwood, Samuel Dugan Sr., and his sons Thomas, Alfred, and Samuel Dugan Jr. came to Indiana, Pennsylvania, operating the Northwood Glass Company there until 1899, when Harry Northwood joined the newly-formed National Glass company combine. In 1903, he moved his operation to Wheeling at the old Hobbs, Brockunier plant, and Thomas Dugan remained at the Indiana plant operating it as the Dugan Glass company.

From 1896 on, several patterns were produced as first Northwood, then National, and finally as Dugan, patterns such as Argonaut Shell/Nautilus, for example. There were many others that have previously been classified as either Northwood or Dugan that are actually Northwood/National/Dugan or even National/Dugan.

In addition, we have certain patterns duplicated by both Jefferson and Northwood with little explanation as to why moulds that were once Jefferson's then became Northwood's. These companies were competitors, but examples of some patterns can be traced to both companies. It is also evident most patterns with a cranberry edging are really Jefferson, not Northwood as once believed.

Every answer raises new questions. Answers come in their own time and at their own pace. One day we'll know most of what we question today and that is what drives us. I learn every day, mostly by contact with other collectors and so, I'm sure, do all of you.

Part I: *Opalescent Glass, 1880 – 1930*

Abalone

Acorn Burrs

Ala-Bock

A balone

Found only in bowls with small handles, the Abalone pattern is believed to be from the Jefferson Glass Company and dates from the 1902 – 1905 period. Colors are blue, white, green, and rarely canary opalescent glass. The design, a series of graduated arcs in column separated by a line of bubble-like dots is nice, but nothing special.

A corn Burrs

Here is another of those well-known Northwood patterns that was made in the 1907 – 09 era in very limited opalescent glass production. Acorn Burrs is found in carnival glass in many shapes such as table sets, water sets, and berry sets. In opalescent glass it is limited to the small berry bowl shape and possibly the larger bowl (though none has been confirmed to date). Opalescent colors seem be just as limited and these small bowls are known in white and blue.

A la-Bock

Similar to the Alhambra pattern, this one also came from Model Flint Glass about 1900. It has been reported in a water set and a rose bowl, but here we have a ruffled bowl shape that was pulled from the same piece as the rose bowl. Colors known in Ala-Bock are blue or vaseline opalescent. Pieces in this pattern seem to be scarce with only the rose bowl showing up in any number.

Alaska

A laska

One of the early Northwood patterns, Alaska dates from 1897 and can be found in a wide range of shapes including table sets, water sets, berry sets, a cruet, banana boat, celery tray, shakers, and bride's basket. The tumblers and shakers are interchangeable with plain Fluted Scrolls and Jackson pieces. Colors are blue, white, vaseline, and emerald green as well as plain and decorated crystal.

A lhambra

Often confused with the Spanish Lace pattern, Alhambra is really an Albany Glass pattern, known in a rose bowl, tumbler, and a reported syrup jug. The confirmation of a tumbler suggests the possibility of a pitcher, but none is reported. Colors in opalescent glass are white, blue, or canary.

A lva

This very impressive oil lamp is found in several variations including a blue opal stripe with frosted base and a vaseline stripe with the same base treatment. Dating to the 1890s, this lamp is quality all the way.

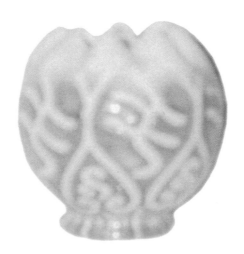

Alhambra

Alva

Arabian Nights

Arched Panel

Argonaut Shell (Nautilus)

Arabian Nights

Dating from 1895 or 1896, this Northwood pattern, while confined to water sets and a syrup, can be found in white, blue, canary, and cranberry opalescent glass. The design (swirls, blossoms, and dots) combines the best of both Spanish Lace and Daisy and Fern and is a very striking pattern.

Arched Panel

When we first showed this 9" bowl, we speculated about the maker but now we know it was made by Jefferson Glass in both large and small berry bowls. There are twelve wide panels around the bowl and the top is scalloped, and there is a many rayed star in the base. Colors are white, green, or blue opalescent. And Heisey made a similar opalescent set called their #300 Peerless pattern.

Argonaut Shell (Nautilus)

Originally a Northwood pattern, the opalescent examples were made by National or by Dugan after Northwood left National. Colors are blue, white, and vaseline and the shapes include water sets, table sets, berry sets, compotes, shakers, novelty bowls, and a cruet.

Ascot

*A*scot
This pattern was made by the Greener Company of England as #262018 in 1895 and found in blue or canary opalescent glass. A complete table set and a biscuit jar with lid are the shapes we've heard about. The design is one of arcs around a circle of file.

*A*stro
Primarily a bowl pattern, Astro was made by the Jefferson Glass Company about 1905. It is a simple design of six circular comet-like rings on a threaded background above three rings of beads that are grouped from the lower center of the bowl upward. Colors are blue, green, white, and canary.

Astro

*A*urora Borealis
Made by the Jefferson Glass Company and dating from 1903, this vase pattern is very typical of stemmed vases in the opalescent glass era. Rising from a notched base, the stem widens with a series of bubbles and scored lines that end in a flame-shaped top. From the sides are three handle-like projections, giving the whole conception a very nautical feeling. Colors are white, green, and blue opalescent.

Aurora Borealis

Autumn Leaves

Baby Coinspot

Ball-foot Hobnail

*A*utumn Leaves

I am very drawn to this beautiful bowl pattern, attributed to the Northwood Company from 1905. The colors reported are green, white, and blue opalescent, and the design is quite good with large, well-veined leaves around the bowl, connected by twisting branches and a single leaf in the bowl's center.

*B*aby Coinspot

While the well-known syrup in Baby Coinspot is from the Belmont Glass Company and dates from 1887, a newer copy is known by Fenton. The 7" vase shown does not appear to be a new item. The glass is thin and light, and the color very soft. It may be that this vase is not American at all but a product of English origin, but I'm sure someone will write me about it. At any rate, it is a very attractive vase and certainly caught my eye.

*B*all-foot Hobnail

So very little is really known about this pattern. It may have been a product of New Brighton Glass Company of New Brighton, Pennsylvania, but this hasn't been confirmed. The date of production seems to be around 1889, and most items are crystal while only a few have opalescence. The distinguishing points of identification seem to be the scallops on the edges and while some pieces do indeed have ball feet, others are collar based!

Banded Neck &
Scale Optic

*B*anded Neck & Scale Optic

This very attractive small vase (5½"
tall) is mould blown and has a pontil mark
on the base. The scale optic pattern is on
the inside and only the banding around
the neck elevates this vase above the ordinary. I suspect it came in the usual colors
but have only seen the white.

*B*arbells

Known only in the bowl shape, this
rather undistinguished pattern has been
credited to the Jefferson Glass Company
in the 1905 – 06 period. The main design
is a series of vertical ribs topped by a
bulls-eye, with a smaller series of
bullseyes below the ribs. Colors are blue,
green, white, and canary.

*B*eaded Base Vase

Very similar to a design by the
Northwood Company and shown in an old
Butler Brothers ad, this attractive JIP vase
is enameled with sprigs of flowers and has
dots painted on the stem and around the
base. If anyone has more information
about this piece, I'd appreciate hearing
from them. I'm sure it came in the usual
opalescent colors.

Barbells

Beaded Base Vase

Beaded Block

Beaded Cable

Beaded Drapes

Beaded Block

From the Imperial Glass Company in 1913, very few opalescent items seem to exist. Imperial was not known for this glass treatment, and any patterns that exist are collectors' treasures. In Beaded Block (called Frosted Block in carnival glass), shapes known are a stemmed creamer, stemmed open sugar reported in vaseline opalescent only, and the small size rose bowl shown, found in lime green opalescent and the beautiful royal blue.

Beaded Cable

This well-known Northwood pattern can be found in several treatments including opalescent, carnival, and custard. In opalescent glass, the colors are blue, green, white, and canary. Both rose bowls and open bowls are from the same mould. The design is simple yet effective and dates from 1904.

Beaded Drapes

This very attractive pattern is thought to be from the Northwood Company although examples with cranberry edging like some Jefferson items can be found. Dating from 1905, the pattern can be found on footed bowls, rose bowls, and banana bowls in blue, green, white, and vaseline.

Beaded Fans

Beaded Fans

Found mostly on footed rose bowls from the same mould as the bowl shown, this pattern is like Shell and Dots minus the dotted base. Colors are white, green, and blue, and the pattern dates from 1905. It has been credited to Northwood, but it is shown in Jefferson Glass ads as #211, so we know it is a Jefferson pattern.

Beaded Fleur de Lis

Attributed to Jefferson Glass, this stemmed compote can be found with the top opened out or turned in like a rose bowl. It was made in the 1906 era in blue, green, and white. The design is quite good, and the base is very distinctive with three wide feet and beaded rings on the stems.

Beaded Moon and Stars

Just why the Fenton people made two patterns so very similar is a mystery; the second, Beaded Stars and Swag, is shown on page 16. Beaded Moon and Stars is often called just Beaded Stars. It came in bowls, a short-stemmed compote, and a banana bowl from the same mould. Colors are blue, green, and white opalescent as well as carnival treatments.

Beaded Ovals in Sand

Originally called Erie, this Dugan/Diamond pattern is very closely related to two other designs from this company. It can be found in water sets, table sets, berry sets, shakers, a cruet, a toothpick holder, and a ruffled small bowl. Found in blue, and white opalescent colors, the pattern was also made in apple green glass, blue, and crystal (sometimes decorated). Opalescent pieces are rather scarce.

Beaded Fleur de Lis

Beaded Moon and Stars

Beaded Ovals in Sand

Beaded Star Medallion

Beaded Stars and Swag

Beads and Bark

Beads and Curlycues

Beaded Star Medallion

Often credited to the Imperial Glass Company in carnival glass, a recent find of marked marigold carnival pieces confirms this to be a Northwood pattern. In opalescent glass, it can be found in white, blue, and green. The pattern dates from the 1909 era and was made for both gas and electric shades.

Beaded Stars and Swag

The opalescent version of this pattern was made by the Fenton Glass Company in 1907. Shapes reported are bowls, rose bowls, and a rare plate. Both the bowl and the plate are known in advertising items (the plate is shown elsewhere) and are very rare. Colors found are white, blue, and green in opalescent glass, crystal, and carnival colors.

Beads and Bark

Shown as early as 1903, this Northwood pattern was made in their "Mosaic" or purple slag treatment, as well as appearing in opalescent colors of white, blue, and canary, and limited amounts of green. Like on so many vases of the time, the theme was a rustic look with tree limbs forming the supports to the base. In the case of Beads and Bark, these supports generate into a bowl that is a series of inverted loops with beaded edging forming three rows of design.

Beads and Curlycues

From the Northwood Company and advertised in Butler Brothers in 1906 in an ad from that company, this scarce short-stemmed piece has an open-edged top, much like that on the Shell and Wild Rose pieces. In the example shown, the top is fanned out evenly all around, but other pieces show a variety of top shapings. Colors in opalescent glass are blue, green, or white, but certainly vaseline may exist.

Beatty Honeycomb

Beatty Honeycomb

Made by Beatty & Sons in Tiffin, Ohio, the Honeycomb pattern dates to 1888 and is also known as Beatty Waffle. Shapes found are table set, water set, berry set, cruet, toothpick holder, celery vase, salt shakers, mustard pot, individual cream and sugar, and the mug shape shown. Colors are white and blue opalescent. Be aware the pattern was reproduced in the 1960s by the Fenton Glass Company in blue and emerald green in vases, baskets, rose bowls, and a covered sugar.

Beatty Rib

The A.J. Beatty & Sons Company originally made glass in Steubenville, Ohio, until they merged with U.S. Glass and moved their operation to Tiffin, Ohio, in 1891. Beatty Rib dates from 1889 and was made in both blue and white in a vast array of shapes including table sets, water sets, berry sets in two shapes, a celery vase, mug, nappies in assorted shapes, salt and pepper shakers, a mustard jar, salt dips, sugar shaker, toothpick holder, finger bowl, match holder, and cracker jar.

Beatty Rib

Beatty Swirl

Like its sister pattern Beatty Rib, this popular design was produced in 1889 in blue, white, and occasionally canary opalescent glass. Shapes known are table sets, water sets, berry sets, syrup, mug, water tray, and celery vase. Other pieces might well have been made including shakers, toothpick holder, cruet, mustard pot, and sugar shaker, so be aware of this possibility.

Beatty Swirl

Beaumont Stripe

Beaumont Swirl

Berry Patch

*B*eaumont Stripe

While one writer thought this was a Northwood pattern, the water pitcher shown has the same shape as that of the Stars and Stripes water set, first made by Hobbs and then by Beaumont in 1899. We believe it was actually made by Beaumont and have so named it, and we'll hear from collectors if we are wrong. The set sits on a tray in the Beatty Swirl pattern.

*B*eaumont Swirl

Percy Beaumont was Harry Northwood's brother-in-law and worked at Northwood before beginning business for himself at the old Elson plant in Martins Ferry, Ohio. On the Swirl pattern shown, the neck of the pitcher is collared or ringed and the striping narrower than most examples. Other colors are white or blue opalescent.

*B*erry Patch

Made by the Jefferson Glass Company as their #261 pattern in 1905, this design seems to be limited to small bowls and plates with a dome base. The design is a simple one, a trailing of vine, leaves, and small berry clusters that ramble around the inside bowl. The example shown is a flattened piece with the edges rolled up and is called a plate by some collectors. The pattern is accented in a goofus treatment of soft coloring, unlike most examples seen. Colors in opalescent are white, blue, and green.

Blackberry

While the pattern is sometimes called Northwood's Blackberry, I have no doubt it was a pattern produced by the Fenton Glass Company. It has been seen mostly in small sauce shapes but occasionally one of these is pulled into a whimsey shape. Colors in opalescent glass are blue, white, green, and a very pretty amethyst (another indication it is Fenton). It can be found in custard and opaque glass, and many times with a goofus treatment.

Blackberry

Blackberry Spray

Very similar to the Blackberry pattern above, this Fenton design has less detail and more sprays. It is found primarily on the hat shape shown and usually in amethyst in opalescent glass, blue opalescent, or white. This same pattern and shape was made in carnival glass during the same time span and 1911 ads are known. Also known in a JIP shape.

Blackberry Spray

Blocked Thumbprint and Beads

While the history of this pattern tends to be confusing mainly because it is only one step in a series of patterns done by the Dugan/Diamond Glass Company over a period of time, the study of two closely designed patterns sets the picture in order. Blocked Thumbprint and Beads and another pattern, Leaf Rosette and Beads (page 85), are very much alike. When you add a Dugan carnival glass item called Fishscale and Beads (page 61) to the picture, you can see that all three patterns came from the same maker. The latter is simply the original Blocked Thumbprint and Beads with an interior pattern of scaling! Opalescent colors are the typical white, blue, and green, but vaseline is a possibility.

Blocked Thumbprint and Beads

Blooms and Blossoms

Blossoms and Palms

Blossoms and Web

Blooms and Blossoms

Also known as Mikado, this Northwood Glass pattern is known in several treatments including frosted glass with enameling, ruby stained with gilt, the flowers painted in an airy transparent coloring, as well as a goofus treatment. In opalescent glass the usual shape is this square-shaped nappy with one handle. It has been called an olive nappy and can be found in white, green, and blue opalescent colors. And if two names aren't enough, it can also be found as Flower and Bud in some books!

Blossoms and Palms

Made by the Northwood Company in both carnival glass and opalescent glass first in 1905, some pieces like the one shown have a goofus treatment. Opalescent colors are white, blue, green, and vaseline, and some pieces have the Northwood trademark. The design consists of three acanthus-like leaves with a stem of flowers and leaves separating each of them.

Blossoms and Web

Advertised in 1906 in a Northwood ad as part of their Egyptian Art Decorated offering, this was one name for the goofus treatment over opalescent items. Blossoms and Web is a difficult pattern to find and is a collector's favorite. Colors are white (sometimes with goofus), blue (scarce), and a very scarce green. The design of six blossoms connected by a webbing of stems with one center blossom is simple but effective.

B lown Diamonds

What an outstanding piece of canary opalescent glass this 11½" tankard pitcher is. The pattern, much like Hobbs Opalescent Diamonds pattern, is all interior. The applied handle is threaded and then twisted. I'm sure this pattern was made in other colors, and I have a strong suspicion it may be English, dating to the 1880s. If so, blue is a strong possibility. If anyone can shed more light on this piece, we'd appreciate knowing.

B lown Drapery

Made by Northwood as part of the National Glass combine in 1903, this very beautiful tankard water set and a companion sugar shaker are mould blown and can be found in white, blue, green, canary, and cranberry opalescent colors. Please compare this set with the later Fenton Drapery set shown on page 49 for a complete understanding of just how this pattern varies from blown to pressed ware. Also, be aware that Blown Drapery has been reproduced in a cruet shape by L.G. Wright.

B lown Twist

Made by Northwood operating as National Glass, this very scarce pattern is known in water sets and a sugar shaker. It dates from 1903, and the colors known are white, blue, canary, green, and cranberry. The handle on the water pitcher has a very unusual twisted look not found on other items in opalescent glass. Please note that the pitcher's mould is the same as that of Blown Drapery (both are blown items). A rare celery vase is known.

Blown Diamonds

Blown Drapery

Blown Twist

Boggy Bayou

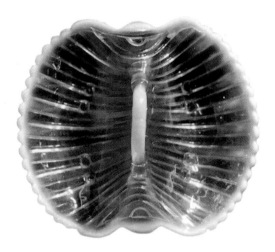

Brideshead

British Flute

*B*oggy Bayou

Often confused with another Fenton pattern called Reverse Drapery, Boggy Bayou is found only on vase shapes. It can be found in opalescent colors of white, green, blue, and amethyst, in sizes from 6" to 13" tall. Production dates from 1907 in both opalescent glass and carnival glass. A Reverse Drapery whimsey vase is shown in the whimsey section, and a comparison of the bases will help distinguish one pattern from the other.

*B*rideshead

Made by Davidson of England (Rd #130643) in 1889, shapes include a water set, table set, celery vase (tall spooner), biscuit jar, 5½" plate, handled fold basket, cake plate on pedestal, fairy lamp, and various bowl shapes. Colors are the usual blue or vaseline opalescent glass. The pattern is a simple one of concave and convex ribbing. Shown is a center-handled sweets dish.

*B*ritish Flute

We believe this pattern is from England, possibly by Davidson. It has a base pontil mark, 16 inside flute or wide panels, and is somewhat square in shape. The top has an interesting three-and-one ruffling much like that done by the Dugan/Diamond Company on some of their glass. This beautiful vaseline opalescent piece is 8" tall and probably came in other colors.

Broken Pillar

*B*roken Pillar (and Reed)

Called Kismet (#909) by some collectors, this pattern was made in 1895 – 1900 era by Model Flint Glass and advertised in many shapes in crystal, decorated colors, and the one stemmed piece in opalescent glass. Colors are white, blue, and vaseline opalescent, and the piece is called a stemmed tray. The design is all exterior with a very patterned stem.

*B*ubble Lattice

This pattern was called Plaid by Marion Hartung but is more commonly known as Bubble Lattice or simply Lattice. It was made in Wheeling by the Hobbs, Brockunier Company in 1889, and can be found in many shapes including water sets, berry sets, table sets, cruets, sugar shakers, syrups, toothpick holders, finger bowls, salt shakers, bowls, and bride's baskets. Colors are blue, white, canary, and cranberry, and the finish was occasionally satinized.

Bubble Lattice

*B*utterfly and Lily Epergne

This very nice one-lily epergne gets its name from the butterfly resting on the top of the metal base, just below the stem and the shape of the lily itself. Of course these lilies were interchangeable so any color can be used. The one shown is the same lily found on the Single Lily Spool piece on page 129.

Butterfly and Lily Epergne

Button Panels

Buttons and Braids

Cabbage Leaf

Button Panels

Shown in Northwood ads in 1902 and later in Dugan/Diamond ads in 1907 but earlier attributed to the Coudersport Tile & Ornamental Glass Company, this is a very plentiful pattern. It i s often confused with Alaska because of their similar designs and is found on bowls and rose bowls, all dome-based and from the same mould. Colors are white, blue, canary, and green, with a seldom seen emerald also known.

Buttons and Braids

Credited to the Jefferson Company, Buttons and Braids dates to 1905 and has been reported in water sets and bowls in blue, green, white, and cranberry opalescent. Tumblers can be either blown or pressed. In addition to the colors listed, there is a strange greenish vaseline that is very much like some of the Everglades pieces credited to Northwood, so this pattern may well have passed from the Jefferson Company to Northwood like others are known to have done.

Cabbage Leaf

Exactly like the Winter Cabbage bowl on page 151, except Cabbage Leaf has three large leaf patterns over the twig-like feet. This piece is usually turned up to form a very neat vase. Both patterns are from the Northwood Company and date from its 1906 – 1907 period of production. Colors in the Cabbage Leaf pattern are white, green, and blue opalescent with canary a possibility.

Calyx

C*alyx*

Made by the Model Flint Glass Company during their association with National and dated to 1899 or a bit later. This scarce vase can be found in crystal, canary opalescent, blue opalescent, white opalescent, as well as opaque colors of blue, green, white, and yellow (shards) as well as some rare decorated opaque examples. A blue opaque vase with green painted leaves is shown in Ron Teal's fine book on Albany Glass.

C*ane Rings*

Found in several books that feature glass from England as a product of the Davidson Company, the pattern shown has never been named as far as we can ascertain, so we've corrected that oversight. We know of bowls, a celery vase, a creamer, and an open sugar in this pattern, but more shapes were probably made. Opalescent colors are blue or vaseline.

Cane Rings

C*arousel*

Made by the Jefferson Glass Company in 1905 as their #264 pattern. Colors in opalescent glass are the usual white, blue, or green, occasionally with a frit decoration. The only shape we've seen is the standard novelty bowl shape, often with varied edge treatments. The design is a simple one that doesn't have much imagination and low appeal to the collector.

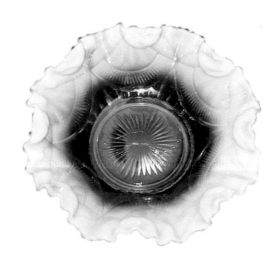

Carousel

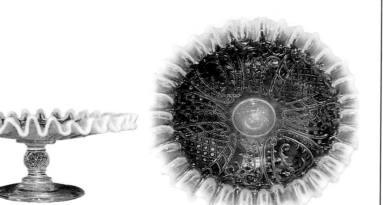

Casbah

Casbah

Very much like Arabian Nights, Rococo, and Arabesque, this very pretty stemmed piece flattened from a compote seems to be English in origin. The stem has a knob that appears to be cross-hatched and the design inside the bowl of the compote is a series of opposing geometrics, four each making up eight panels. Shown in white, there is probably a blue and maybe a canary example out there. The design dates this piece to the 1890s.

Cashews

Cashews

Attributed to the Northwood Glass Company, we suspect it was later continued by Dugan/Diamond. Shapes are bowls, plates, and a nice rose bowl, all from the same mould. Colors are white, blue, and green opalescent with some white examples found with a goofus treatment.

Cherry

Cherry

Made by Bakewell, Pears and Company about 1870, the Cherry pattern was made in crystal as well as opalescent glass in many shapes including a scarce plate, goblet, berry set, table set, stemmed wine, open and covered compotes, and novelty bowls of several shapes. The cherry design is very realistic and the leaves form arcs.

Cherry Panel (Dugan Cherry)

Better known in carnival glass, this Dugan/Diamond pattern is often seen in peach opalescent glass. Other carnival glass colors are amethyst and marigold. In opalescent glass reported colors are white, blue, and canary. The example shown has a goofus treatment with the cherries done in red and the leaves in gold. Production dates to 1907 and the only shape reported in opalescent glass is the three-footed bowl, often shaped in a variety of ways.

Cherub Epergne

Here is another of the very attractive metal epergnes that held opalescent lilies. This one shows a cherub supporting a potted plant that spreads its leaves to hold a Dahlia Twist lily, made by Jefferson Glass. Jefferson seemed to use more of these metal holders than most glass makers and each one is a treasure to find.

Chippendale

This very pretty pattern was a product of George Davidson and Company, England, and dates to 1887. Shapes known are baskets, compotes, and tumblers, so I suspect a jug or pitcher of some shape was made. Colors are blue and canary and both are top notch as the photo clearly shows.

Christmas Pearls

Occasionally called Beaded Panel (it isn't the same as the Beaded Panels pattern often called Opal Open), this quite rare and beautiful pattern is most likely a Jefferson Glass design that dates from 1901 – 1903. The only shapes reported are the cruet shown and a salt shaker. The colors known so far are blue, white, and green opalescent.

Cherry Panel

Cherub Epergne

Chippendale

Christmas Pearls

Christmas Snowflake

Christmas Trees

*Chrysanthemum
(Base) Swirl*

Christmas Snowflake

Originally a Hobbs, Brockunier pattern, Christmas Snowflake was a lamp pattern produced by that company in 1891. In 1888, Northwood began production in water sets (both plain and ribbed) as well as a cruet and possibly a vase. In 1980 a reproduction was made by L.G. Wright of the plain water set, as well as new shapes (sugar shaker, barber bottle, basket, rose bowls in two sizes, syrup, milk pitcher, cruet, brides bowl, and a creamer). The original lamps were made in three sizes in blue, white, and cranberry. The Northwood water set was made in the same colors and the cruet in white only.

Christmas Trees

Show is a blown 9¼" "smoke shade," used in the oil lamp era to shield rooms from lamp soot. The treatment is Rubina Verde (page 118), a process of combined vaseline and cranberry (here with opalescence). Hobbs, Brockunier introduced this treatment in 1884 but we have no proof this rare, rare shade is from that company. We would appreciate any information about this piece and thank the Sandemans for sharing this rare find.

Chrysanthemum (Base) Swirl

First made at the Buckeye Glass Company of Martins Ferry, Ohio, this design became one produced by the Northwood Company in a speckled finish. Buckeye production dates to 1890 in white, blue, and cranberry, sometimes with a satin finish. Shapes are water sets, table sets, berry sets, a cruet, syrup, sugar shaker, toothpick holder, salt shaker, finger bowl, celery vase, mustard, and a beautiful straw holder with lid. The speckled treatment was patented by Northwood and except for this look, the shapes are the same.

Chrysanthemum Swirl Variant

Chrysanthemum Swirl Variant

Here is a very scarce variant pattern, credited to the Northwood Company by some. It has even been called a mystery variant. In size and make-up, the tankard pitcher is much like Ribbed Opal Lattice, also credited to Northwood from 1888; however if you examine the color of the pitcher here, you will find it anything but typical of that company. It isn't blue or even green, but a very strong teal. It can also be found in white and cranberry. It is possible the design was first made elsewhere and Northwood produced later versions.

Circled Scroll

Made in 1904 by the Dugan Glass Company and continued when the factory became Dugan/Diamond, this pattern is found in carnival glass, apple green glass, and opalescent glass. Shapes are a water set, berry set, table set, cruet set, jelly compote, and salt shakers but not in all colors or all treatments. In carnival there is also a whimsey vase, pulled from a tumbler. Opalescent colors are white, blue, and green.

Circled Scroll

Cleopatra's Fan (Northwood's Shell)

After a series of names, the latest seems to be "Cleopatra's Fan," so we'll settle on that one. Known in white, blue, and green opalescent glass, this pattern is actually a product of Dugan/Diamond and was never a part of the Northwood line. It is quite scarce and collectible.

Cleopatra's Fan

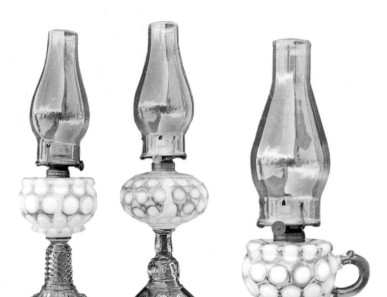

Coin Dot Lamps

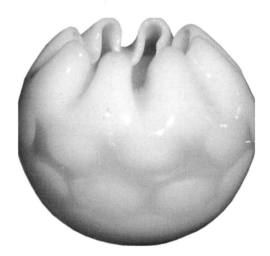

Coinspot (Jefferson)

Coinspot (Northwood)

C oin Dot Lamps

Shown are three very distinctive oil lamps in the Coin Dot pattern. The largest lamp is called Inverted Thumbprint and Fan base and dates to 1890. It can be also found in blue opal. The other table lamp is called Chevron Base and is shown in a 1893 U.S. Glass ad, made by King Glass of Pittsburgh. I strongly suspect the small hand lamp was from the same company since they have the same font shape. I'm sure other colors were made in both of these.

C oinspot (Jefferson)

I believe this previously unreported rose bowl was made by Jefferson from their salad bowl (Jefferson's #83). This company also made the water set (#180) in white, blue, green, and cranberry which was later copied by the Fenton Company. Please note the base which has been ground first.

C oinspot (Northwood)

Shown is the Northwood water pitcher with the star-crimp top. These water sets were made at the Indiana, Pa., plant and production was probably continued when Dugan took over the plant. Butler Brothers catalog ads show this pitcher in 1903 – 1904 from the Northwood/National production. Colors are white, blue, green, and cranberry.

Coinspot Syrup

Coinspot Syrup

While it is, at best, difficult to distinguish some moulds of one company from those of another, I truly believe the syrup shown is from the West Virginia Glass Company and the same shape can be found in their Polka Dot items where the dots are colored rather than opalescent. At any rate, I'm sure these pieces were made in white, blue, cranberry, and possibly other colors since some Coinspot items are also found in green, amber, vaseline, amberina, rubina, and even amethyst.

Coinspot Water Bottle

In addition to all the other Coinspot items we've shown, I just couldn't resist showing this very scarce water bottle shape. The glass is very lightweight and delicate and it has been seen in cranberry opalescent glass, as well as this white example. While I haven't been able to confirm the maker of this item, I'm confident it is old and quite scarce.

Coinspot Water Bottle

Colonial Stairsteps

Although mostly found on this toothpick holder shape, a breakfast set consisting of a creamer and sugar is also known. Colors are crystal and blue opalescent only and although the breakfast set has been reported with the Northwood trademark, none has been seen to date so the attribution is a bit shaky at this time.

Colonial Stairsteps

Commonwealth

Compass

Concave Columns

Commonwealth

Shown is a standard tumbler, 3½" tall, with no pattern whatsoever. We believe this piece was used like the Universal tumbler and could be put with various pitchers to form a water set. Colors are blue or white opalescent, but certainly other treatments were made from this same mould and these include crystal, opaque, and carnival glass. Opalescent pieces are known to have been enameled also.

Compass

Made by the Dugan/Diamond factory primarily as an exterior pattern on their Heavy Grape carnival glass pieces, this pattern comes into its own in opalescent glass where it can be found on both 9" and 5½" bowls, as well as on 10" and 6½" plates. Some of these pieces are marked with the Diamond-D mark and opalescent colors are white, green, or blue. The pattern is a good one with eight overlapping arcs and a marie (base) design of oversecting stars.

Concave Columns (#617)

As stated elsewhere (see Pressed Coinspot), this pattern was originally called #617 in a 1901 National Glass catalog and was later continued by Dugan/Diamond Glass in an ad assortment in the compote shape. For some strange reason, the vase has become known as Concave Columns. The compote in opalescent glass is known as Pressed Coinspot and in carnival glass is simply called Coinspot. Shapes from the same mould are vases, compotes, goblets, and a stemmed banana boat. Colors in opalescent glass are white, blue, green, and canary.

Conch and Twig

Conch and Twig

Made by Burtles, Tate and Company of England in 1885 with RD #39807, this is another of those marvelous wall pocket vases the British made in opalescent glass. This one has the very natural look of a seashell with a twig-like holder or hanger. Colors are the usual English ones of blue or vaseline opalescent glass.

Constellation

Shown in a 1914 Butler Brothers ad for Dugan/Diamond Glass Company, this very scarce compote was reported to be available in both white and blue opalescent. Originally the mould for this piece was the S-Repeat goblet (the pattern was originally called National and was a product of Northwood/National Glass that dated to 1903). When Dugan obtained the National moulds, the exterior pattern became S-Repeat and the goblet was turned into a compote with a pattern on the interior called Constellation. In addition to the few opalescent items, many shapes were made in colored crystal with gilding, as well as a few shapes in carnival glass including the compote where the S-Repeat exterior is known as Seafoam! Another example of name complication that plagues collectors.

Constellation

Contessa

Made by Greener & Company in England in 1890 and bearing the RD number 160244, this hobnailed pattern can be found in several shapes that include a pitcher, a two-piece footed breakfast set consisting of creamer and open sugar, and the handled basket shown. Opalescent colors include blue, canary, and the rare amber shown.

Contessa

Coral

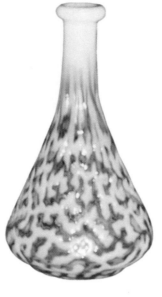

Coral Reef

Cornith

Cornucopia

Coral

Found only on bowls with odd open work around the edging, the Coral pattern may well be a product of the Jefferson Company. Colors are the usual: white, blue, green, and vaseline. While it has the same name as a Fenton carnival glass pattern, the design is far different.

Coral Reef

While most collectors have lumped this pattern with Seaweed, it truly is a different pattern and it took a letter from a collector and an article by John D. Sewell to set me straight on this pattern. Seaweed has branches and distinct round dots while Coral Reef (Mr. Sewell's name) has a rambling line pattern with square-type extensions rather than dots. Coral Reef can be found in bitters bottles, barber bottles (round or square), finger bowls, lamps in four sizes including a mini night lamp, a stemmed oil lamp, a finger lamp, and a stemmed finger lamp.

Cornith

After the last edition of this book, we learned this 11" vase is not Westmoreland but was produced by U.S. Glass as their #15021 pattern. It was made in both white and blue opalescent glass. The design has twelve ribs that begin just above the base.

Cornucopia

Made by Northwood in 1905, this novelty vase with handles can be found in white, blue, or green opalescent glass. Production continued for at least two years and despite there being rumors of this piece in carnival glass, none has ever surfaced. The design is almost like a wicker basket weave that rolls at the bottom to rest on a decorative base.

C orn Vase

Despite having been reproduced by Wright Glass in the 1960s, this beautiful Dugan pattern is a collector's dream. Dugan made it in 1905 in white, blue, vaseline, and a rare green, as well as a super-rare marigold carnival. The mould work is fantastic and the open husks show real glassmaking skill.

C orolla

Probably made after National Glass took over the Model Flint factory at Albany, Indiana, this pattern has appeared in the vase shape only. Colors are white, canary, or blue opalescent, and opaque pieces in white, blue, canary, and green glass. Production was likely in the 1900 – 1902 time frame, and some pieces have been found (shards) at the factory site. Production was small, for a short period of time we suspect.

C oronation

Here is another opalescent pattern from England, named by Heacock, and seen in both blue and canary opalescent glass. Shapes reported are a tankard pitcher, a tumbler, a creamer, and a stemmed open sugar, but we feel sure other shapes were made. The design is one of cane panels, separated by ovals of plain glass and topped by a fan shape of three elongated hearts.

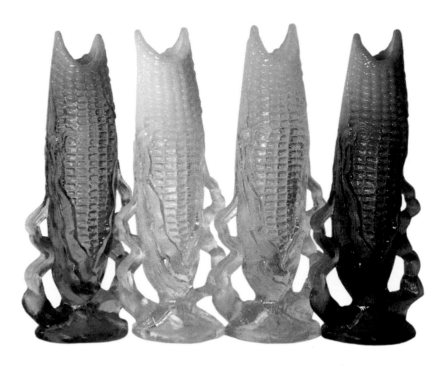

Corn Vase

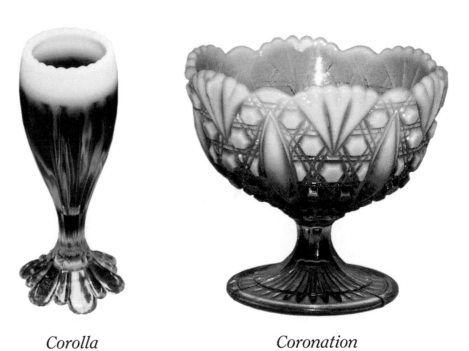

Corolla   *Coronation*

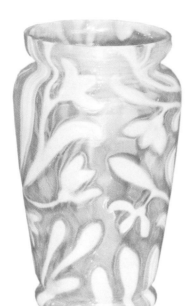

Crocus

Crown Jewels

Curtain Optic

*C*rocus

Since we showed this fine vase in the last edition of this book, we've learned of an example that was marked "Made in Czechoslovakia," so we can now say with authority where this vase was made. It stands 6½" tall and has a 2¾" base diameter and in design is much like the Daffodil pattern that was made first by Northwood and then by Dugan/Diamond. The example shown is a strong turquoise color.

*C*rown Jewels

Here's another pattern from England, found on blue or canary opalescent glass. Shapes reported include a tankard pitcher on a pedestal base, a tall tumbler, a plate, and the oval platter shown. The design is a simple one of four opposing petals or ovals with a starburst in the center of each. These groupings are arranged in a criss-cross style.

*C*urtain Optic

Fenton began making this very pretty design in 1922 and continued for several years, adding a medium wide striped opalescent pattern called Rib Optic. These patterns were made in several pitcher sizes and shapes along with iced tea tumblers, handled tall tumblers, and handled mugs. Even a two-piece guest set (small bedside pitcher and tumbler) can be found. Usually, the handles on both pitchers and mugs were of a darker glass. Some of these opalescent items were iridized.

Cyclone

Cyclone

If you will examine the base, stem, and twig legs of the Beads and Bark piece and the design of the body of the Ocean Shell pattern, you will see the two have been combined on this rare, rare Northwood vase shape. Only two are reported, both in vaseline. One is marked "Northwood", the other isn't. The examples known are 7½" tall and we suspect both white and blue opalescent glass examples were made.

Daffodil

Shown in a couple of 1906 ads in a Lyon Brothers catalog along with other Northwood pattern water sets, it seems this pattern was continued by the Dugan Company after Northwood left the Indiana, Pa., factory. The pitchers are in two shapes, bulbous or a slimmer tankard, and colors known are white, canary, green, and blue. There is also a variant pitcher which has fewer blossoms and foliage that appears to be Northwood's also.

Daffodil

Daffodils Oil Lamp

While both Northwood and Dugan/Diamond made this pattern in water sets, we believe this oil lamp shape was made by only Northwood about 1904 or 1905. Correspondence from their factory indicates they were making opalescent glass lamps, some with goofus base decorations and others with ruby staining on the base. Shown is a white opalescent glass table lamp with goofus on the base.

*Daffodils Oil
Lamp*

Daffodils Vase

Dahlia Twist

Dahlia Twist Epergne

*D*affodils Vase

While it is hard to say whether some pieces in this pattern came from Northwood or Dugan/Diamond, we believe this vase is from the latter and one of their pitcher moulds without the handle. The vase shown is 5½" tall, 4½" across the top, and has a base diameter of 4¾". Colors are white, blue, or vaseline opalescent.

*D*ahlia Twist

Made by the Jefferson Glass Company around 1905, Dahlia Twist was originally Jefferson's #207 pattern. It is a typical cone-shaped vase on a circular base with a flared and ruffled top. The real interest comes in the ribbing that is twisted against an interior optic that runs in the opposite direction. Colors are the typical white, green, and blue opalescent.

*D*ahlia Twist Epergne

I am thrilled to show this very beautiful epergne as it was originally sold. Most collectors believe this Jefferson Glass lily had a glass dome-based bowl as a holder, but the lily was made expressly for decorative metal holders as shown in ads of the day. Most were silvered but a few were gilded as the one shown. The lily came in the usual opalescent colors and a similar lily and metal holder in the Fishnet pattern was sold by the Dugan/Diamond Company.

Daisy and Button

Daisy and Button

Believed to be from Edward Bolton (Oxford Lane Glass Works) in England, this pattern and shape were later copied by Hobbs in non-opalescent colors and even later made by the Fenton Company for L.G. Wright. Both English and Hobbs productions date to the 1880s and the reproductions for Wright began in the late 1930s. The piece shown is called an oval crown bowl or a bun tray. Old ones are found in blue or canary opalescent glass, as are the reproductions.

Daisy and Drape

Well known to carnival glass collectors, this Northwood pattern stands 6½" tall. In design it much resembles a U.S. Glass pattern called Vermont and may well have been a Northwood copy. Nevertheless, this is the first known Daisy and Drape vase in opalescent glass and I can't begin to tell you just how rare and important a find it is. We can only hope someone had the good sense to produce other colors. A blue would be a super find.

Daisy and Drape

Daisy and Fern

Made at several factories including West Virginia Glass, Northwood (alone and as part of National), and the Dugan Company, this pattern was later reproduced and sold by L.G. Wright as early as 1939. Colors for old items include white, blue, green, and cranberry. New items were made in white, blue, canary (not found in old pieces), and cranberry. Be especially cautious about rose bowls and barber bottles as well as cruets. All have been reproduced.

Daisy and Fern

Daisy and Fern
(Apple Blossom Mould)

Daisy and Greek Key

Daisy and Plume

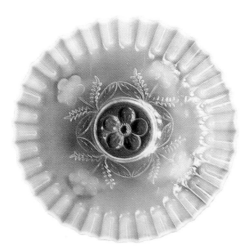

Daisy Dear

Daisy and Fern (Apple Blossom Mould)

Never reproduced like many other Daisy and Fern items, Northwood's Apple Blossom Mould line can be found in several shapes including a spooner (shown), creamer, sugar, and night lamp. Colors are blue, white, and cranberry. The spooner shape also doubled as a pickle caster insert.

Daisy and Greek Key

Since the last edition of this book, we've learned Daisy and Greek Key is probably an English pattern, possibly from Davidson Glass. The design is found only on small footed square sauces in white, blue, or green but since canary (or vaseline) is usually found in opalescent glass from England, that has to be a possibility.

Daisy and Plume

While this famous design was made for years under the Northwood/National banner, the example shown comes from the Dugan Company, despite having no holes in the legs. The mould work is excellent and there is no Northwood marking. Colors are green, white, and blue opalescent glass and carnival glass. Dugan ads date from 1907 on this footed rose bowl.

Daisy Dear

Made by the Dugan/Diamond Company and well known to carnival glass collectors, this pattern is exterior only and not very imaginative. It is found in opalescent glass in white, green, or blue, in bowls of all shapes, and plates like the ruffled example shown. Production began in 1907. The pattern shows four blossom-and-leaf sprigs around the bowl and a daisy design on the marie.

Daisy in Criss-Cross

Reported to be a product of Beaumont Glass around 1895 and found in water sets as well as a syrup, this scarce pattern is found in white, cranberry, blue, and sapphire blue in opalescent glass. The water pitcher has a ring-neck shaping as does the syrup. Tumblers are flat based and straight sided. A very collectible pattern but not easy to find.

Daisy May

Made by the Dugan/Diamond Company, this very attractive nappy is a kissin' cousin to the Leaf Rays pattern found in carnival glass. On Leaf Rays the pattern is interior while on Daisy May the design is all exterior and shows through the glass nicely. It has been shown in 1909 ads and the few examples that I've seen are blue opalescent despite being advertised in white also.

Daisy Wreath

We are extremely pleased to show this very rare item from the Westmoreland Company. It is usually found in carnival glass on a milk glass base, but here we have a rich blue glass with opalescent edges. The bowl is 9" in diameter and is the only example in opalescent glass I've seen without iridescence.

Davidson Pearline Epergne

Standing 14" tall, this dramatic four lily epergne sits on a very deep well-bowl with the same feet Davidson used on other items (see Lady Caroline pattern). We believe this epergne was made in blue pearline also and possibly white which Davidson called "Moonshine Pearline." The glass is thin and very fine quality.

Daisy in Criss-Cross

Daisy May

Daisy Wreath

Davidson Pearline Epergne

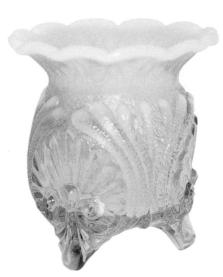

Davidson Shell

Desert Garden

Diamond and Daisy

Davidson Shell

Made by the George Davidson & Company Glass Works of Gateshead, England in 1889, this small footed piece (3¼" tall) is called a spill vase (spills are long wooden matches) or a posey vase. The piece shown has the Davidson Lion-on-Rampart trademark. It can be found in blue or vaseline opalescent glass as well as opaque pieces in blue, white, or black.

Desert Garden

This novelty dome-base bowl pattern can be found in white, blue, or green opalescent glass. The design of three sets of leaves bracketing a stylized blossom with a stippled background isn't very imaginative but does fill most of the available space. The example shown, like most, has a ribbon-candy edging that adds to the appearance. The maker hasn't been determined, but I lean toward Dugan/Diamond.

Diamond and Daisy (Caroline)

Ads in a 1909 Butler Brothers catalog identify this pattern as part of the Intaglio line from the Dugan Company. It is clearly shown in a handled basket shape, so we know at least two shapes were made. Dugan first advertised the Intaglio line in 1905, and it included painted plain crystal as well as blue, green, and white opalescent. The pattern of Diamond and Daisy is very similar to the Wheel and Block pattern. Known as "Caroline" in carnival glass.

*Diamond and Oval
Thumbprint*

Diamond and Oval Thumbprint

This very attractive design, found only on the vase shape, is from the Jefferson Glass Company, circa 1904. It can be found in white, blue, or green opalescent glass and may vary in size from 6" tall to 14".

Diamond Maple Leaf

Attributed to the Dugan Glass Company (Dugan/Diamond), this hard to find two-handled bon-bon can be found in green, white, and blue opalescent. The design shows rather realistic maple leaves flanked by very flowing scroll designs that give the piece a real artistic look. Diamond Maple Leaf dates from 1909.

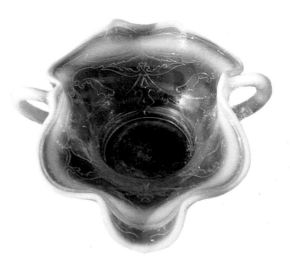

Diamond Maple Leaf

Diamond Optic

I know very little about this attractive piece except it is from England. I base this on the finish and shaping. It may be known by another name also, but I felt this name summed up the configuration as well as any. The diamond pattern is all on the inside and runs from the outer rim to a middle diameter above the stem. It can be found in white opalescent also and may well have been made in canary or vaseline.

Diamond Optic

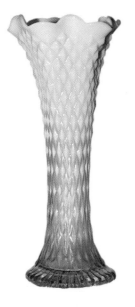

Diamond Point

Diamond Point and Fleur-de-Lis

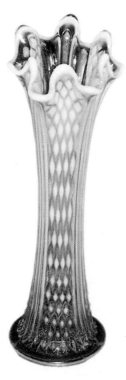

*Diamond Point
Columns*

Diamond Pyramid

*D*iamond Point

Found only on the vase shape, this Northwood pattern dates from 1907 and can be found in white, blue, and green opalescent glass, and many carnival glass colors. Sizes range from 8" to a lofty 14" that has been swung to reach that size.

*D*iamond Point and Fleur-de-Lis

Made by the Northwood Company and illustrated in their 1906 ads, most pieces can be found with the Northwood trademark. Found in novelty bowls that have a collar base, some shapes have been whimsied and a nut bowl shape is known. Colors in opalescent glass are white, blue, or green, according to the ads but certainly vaseline is a possibility.

*D*iamond Point Columns

While many carnival glass collectors are familiar with this pattern and associate it with the Imperial Glass Company of Bellaire, Ohio, it was also a product of the Fenton Company and is shown in Butler Brothers ads with other Fenton patterns. In opalescent glass, only the vase has been reported, and I am very happy to show an example of this rarity. This opalescent piece stands 12" tall and was made in 1907.

*D*iamond Pyramid

We hadn't seen this small, four-footed bowl until recently. The pattern is unlisted as far as we know but certainly looks English and probably came from Sowerby, so we've taken the liberty of naming it. The color is a strong vaseline but it was probably made in blue as well and possibly in other shapes also. Anyone with information on this pattern is urged to contact us.

Diamonds

Diamonds

Made by Hobbs, Brockunier & Company, this cute bud vase dates from 1888. In addition to being opalescent, it has an added coralene decoration of flowers and leaves in the tiny glass beading that was so popular at the time. Usually found on water pitchers (two shapes) in cranberry, this vase is a real rarity. It is only 5" tall.

Diamond Spearhead

Made by the Northwood Glass Company as part of their line when they were part of National, this was their #22 pattern, made in 1901. It can be found in crystal as well as opalescent glass. Shapes include a table set, water set, goblet, berry set, toothpick holder, mug, syrup, shakers, decanter, jelly compote, tall fruit compote, cup and saucer, 10" plate, water carafe, relish tray, and spittoon whimsey. The water pitcher and the creamer are found in more than one size. Colors are green, white, vaseline, blue, and sapphire blue in opalescent glass.

Diamond Spearhead

Diamond Stem

Now known to be made in three sizes, 6½", 8½", and 10½", this very scarce vase from Model Flint dates to about 1900. Colors are canary opalescent, blue opalescent, green opalescent, transparent green, and blue, green, or white opaque pieces. Vases are found in straight, ruffled or flared tops, as well as the familiar turned-in top. The name comes from the knob on the stem that has diamond facets.

Diamond Stern

Diamond Wave

Dogwood Drape

Dolly Madison

Diamond Wave

First thought to be English or European glass, the origin of this unique pattern remains blurred. The covered pitcher has shown up in amethyst opalescent as well as the cranberry coloring previously known. Now we add a 4¾" vase to the mix. All pieces are mould blown with very rich opalized work.

Dogwood Drape

I want to thank all those who pointed out the pattern I called Palm Rosette was really Dogwood Drape and so I am joining them here and now as they should be. The plate and the compote are still the only shapes we've heard about and we still suspect the design is English although we have no proof. Only white opalescent glass has been reported to date.

Dolly Madison

Originally called #271, this pattern by the Jefferson Glass Company was first produced in 1907 and can be found in crystal and blue glass, and opalescent colors of white, blue, and green. Shapes include water sets, table sets, berry sets, plates, and novelty bowls. The design uses panels with flowers, stems, and leaves in every other one.

Dolphin

Dolphin

Originally made by the Northwood Company as early as 1902, this beautiful compote has been widely reproduced in all colors, so buy only what you are confident with. Colors are white, blue, and vaseline. The older compotes have a stronger color and better glass clarity but those are about the only differences.

Dolphin and Herons

From Model Flint Glass of Albany, Indiana, this very sought pattern is known in opalescent glass in a shallow compote shape or a flattened card tray shape. A very rare vase is known in crystal. Opalescent pieces are found in white, blue, a rare cranberry, and canary. All pieces are from the same mould with the stem showing a dolphin turning back on its tail and herons and fauna on the bowl of the piece.

Dolphin and Herons

Dolphin Petticoat

Shards of these lovely candlesticks have been found at the Indiana, Pennsylvania, factory dump site and the pattern is shown in a National Glass ad, so we know the Northwood Company made these while a part of the National Combine. Colors are white, blue, and canary. The mould work is outstanding, as is the design.

Dolphin Petticoat

Dot Optic

Double Dolphin

Double Greek Key

Double Stem Rose

Dot Optic

Made by the Fenton Glass Company as early as 1910 in amethyst opalescent items, the pitcher shown dates to 1921. It is a tankard shape but the same design can be found in bulbous styles as well. Dot Optic is characterized by dots that recede into the glass and differ from the similar Coin Dot pattern in this respect. Colors found are white, blue, vaseline, and green. Shapes include pitchers, tumblers, vases, bowls, and handled tumblers.

Double Dolphin

This is Fenton's #1533 pattern and the opalescent production was very limited. Dating to the 1920s, colors I've verified are blue or white (Fenton calls this French opalescent). This dolphin design was, of course, one of the company's favorites and has been used in many shapes and sizes for 75 years.

Double Greek Key

First a product of the Nickel Plate Glass Company of Fostoria, Ohio, and later by U.S. Glass after 1892. Shapes include a table set, berry set, water set, a celery vase, toothpick holder, mustard pot, syrup, pickle dish, and shakers. Colors in opalescent glass are white or blue, but the pattern can also be found in plain crystal. A very collectible pattern.

Double Stem Rose

While this famous Dugan/Diamond pattern is very well-known in carnival glass, the example shown is the first in opalescent glass I've seen. It has to be quite rare. The pattern dates from 1910, and I'm sure this bowl was an early product. As you can see, it has the very typical Dugan one-two-one crimp and may well show up in other opalescent colors including blue and green, and each of these would be equally rare.

Drapery (Fenton)

Drapery (Fenton)

While the Blown Drapery pattern was made at the Northwood Company, the Fenton example is mould-blown and dates to 1910, five years later than Northwood's. In addition, the Fenton version has a shorter, ball-shaped pitcher while the Northwood version is tankard-shaped. Fenton Drapery colors are the usual white, blue, and green opalescent with amethyst being a possibility.

Drapery (Northwood)

Sometimes called Northwood's Drapery, this interesting pattern dates from 1904 and usually is marked. Colors are white and blue opalescent, often with gold decorated edges and ribbing. Shapes known are table sets, water sets, berry sets, and some novelty items including a rose bowl. Some of the shapes were carried over into carnival glass production; these include rose bowls, candy dishes (from the same mould), and the vase shape.

Drapery (Northwood)

Drapery Rose Bowl

Here is the rose bowl shape in Northwood's Drapery pattern and as you can see, the design is more like the tumbler or pitcher than the vase which has the bands extending over the base. The rose bowl was made in carnival glass also and the same mould was used to make a candy bowl by turning out the rim. Colors in opalescent glass are white and blue, but we suspect green was also made.

Drapery Rose Bowl

Drapery Vase

Dugan Coinspot

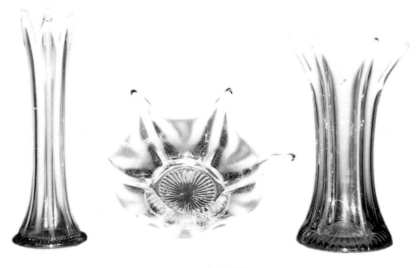

Dugan's #1013

*D*rapery Vase

If you will examine the Drapery pattern made by the Northwood Company, you will see this vase is theirs also and was made in several types of glass including opalescent, carnival, and crystal. Some people call this vase a whimsey but they were literally made by the hundreds, so they are not true whimsey pieces. Colors are blue, white, green, and canary.

*D*ugan Coinspot

Made from 1906 to 1909 and shown in a Dugan/Diamond company catalog in 1907 as their #900 lemonade set, this very nicely shaped pitcher was made in decorated glass as well as opalescent glass in white, blue, or green. The almost-melon ribbing of the lower portion of the pitcher is the distinctive characteristic. The ad shows pitchers and tumblers on a tray that probably didn't match.

*D*ugan's #1013 (Wide Rib)

Shown in 1905 Butler Brothers ads along with other Dugan/Diamond products, this nice vase hasn't much in the way of design but is long on opalescence. It is often very widely flared at the top with opal running from the flames down between the ribs. Colors reported are blue, green, white, and canary, but I've never seen the canary. This vase was also made in carnival glass, often twisted. Shown are two sizes of the vase as well as a bowl whimsey from the same mould.

Dugan's Acorn Intaglio

Like the Intaglio Grape and the other patterns in the Dugan Intaglio line, this one is on white opalescent glass with a goofus treatment given to the pattern by applying it to the exterior within the recesses of the intaglio pattern. Here we have a nearly square bowl that measures 10" across. The glass is very heavy and well designed. Thanks to John E. Wray for this piece.

Dugan's Daisy Intaglio (Western Daisy)

In 1905 the Dugan Glass Company began producing a line of glass in crystal and opalescent white that had a goofus treatment. The following year they added colors to this line. It was advertised in 1909 as their intaglio line and it included the pattern shown, which is known in carnival glass as Western Daisy and in opalescent glass as Daisy Intaglio. Colors are blue, green, and white, often with a goofus treatment.

Dugan's Diamond Compass (Dragon Lady)

As I said in the first edition of this book, this pattern has been confused with two other Dugan patterns, namely Reflecting Diamonds and Compass. There are differences and if you will compare the photos, you will see changes in both the collar base (marie) and the pattern designs. Green and blue, and white opalescent are the reported colors, but blue opalescent was surely made.

Dugan's Acorn Intaglio

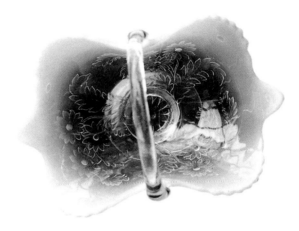

Dugan's Daisy Intaglio

Dugan's Diamond Compass

Dugan's Hexagon Base

Dugan's Honeycomb

Dugan's Intaglio

Dugan's Hexagon Base

This very pretty Dugan vase with the hex base and the jack-in-the-pulpit turned top, stands 7½" tall. The coloring is very good and the mould work excellent. This vase was made in white and green opalescent, and perhaps with a ruffled top. It dates from the 1907 – 1910 period. Two sizes are known.

Dugan's Honeycomb

The mould for this pattern was made in 1905 or 1906 and is usually found in a rose bowl shape in carnival glass. A few pieces have surfaced in speckled treatments called Japanese or Pompeian, but only the bowl shown in white opalescent and one green opalescent bowl are known in this treatment (both have a ribbon-candy edge). We strongly suspect blue and vaseline opalescent examples may have been made, but all colors are rare in this pattern.

Dugan's Intaglio

Designed in 1904 for a line of mostly goofus ware, Dugan's Intaglio designs were primarily fruit patterns (very rare examples of flowers and birds exist) that had a gold and colored treatment to the leaves and fruits while the rest of the glass remained crystal. Fruits found are cherries, grapes, strawberries, and plums, while flower patterns were mostly roses and poppies. Not all of these pieces had opalescence but a few did; we are showing a very pretty Cherries bowl which had red fruit and gilt leaves.

Dugan's Intaglio Grape

As part of the Dugan Intaglio line, this beautiful 13" chop plate can be found with or without opalescent treatment and has been seen with gilding and enamel work. Many of the patterns in this line, some shown elsewhere in this book, have been found in colors of green or blue opalescent and it is possible this grape pattern may have been made in colors, too. The pattern is all exterior and is intaglio.

Dugan's Junior
(Jack-in-the-Pulpit Vase)

If you compare this Dugan vase to the stemmed Dugan jack-in-the-pulpit on page 52, you will see both have a wide ribbed exterior and are shaped exactly the same. This one is flat and measures 4½" tall while the hex-based one measures 7½" tall. The Junior is known in the usual opalescent colors of white, blue, and green.

Dugan's Olive Nappy

In a Butler Brothers 1906 ad, this piece is called a fancy handled olive and was listed available in white, blue, and green opalescent glass from the Dugan/Diamond Company. It measures some 4¾" across from handle to opposite edge and is on a flat base. Since there is no interior or exterior design, it relies on shape and glass finish for whatever appeal it has.

Dugan's Intaglio Grape

Dugan's Junior

Dugan's Olive Nappy

Dugan's Peach Intaglio

Dugan's Strawberry Epergne

Dugan's Strawberry Intaglio

Dugan's Peach Intaglio

Like the other patterns in the Intaglio line, this design of peaches is a companion piece to the grape plate that is also 13" in diameter. Notice this piece still has the goofus treatment as well as opalescence and is just a super exterior design. Intaglio pieces came in all shapes including plates, baskets, bowls, and compotes and in many sizes.

Dugan's Strawberry Epergne

Here is the first reported opalescent example of the Dugan pattern. The 9" single lily is missing but the center hole where it fits is obvious. Found primarily in amethyst carnival glass, the bowl is dome based and measures approximately 9" across. There are three groups of strawberries and leaves that point toward the bowl's center. The missing lily is solid glass halfway up with a design of rows of dots until diamond criss-crossing begins. At the top is another row of dots.

Dugan's Strawberry Intaglio

Like the other intaglio patterns made by the Dugan/Diamond Company beginning in 1905 and continuing for several years, this pattern was decorated with the goofus treatment on white opalescent glass. Shown is a rather large bowl but the same pattern is found on a stemmed 10" fruit holder.

*E*llen

We've been able to learn little about this beautiful 5" vase. It is of very thick, clear glass and has six wide panels on the exterior that extend from below the rim to the scalloped base. The opalescence is quite heavy and rich. I've seen this vase in white and green but expect a blue exists. Unable to find a name, I've called it Ellen in honor of my mother.

*E*lson Dew Drop

Once thought to be from Northwood, we know this was made in 1887 by the Elson firm in colored glass, crystal, satin colors of blue or amber, and opalescent glass in white. The Elson Company was reorganized in 1893 as West Virginia Glass and this was their #90 pattern. Shapes in opalescent glass are a table set and the tall celery vase shown, as well as a berry set, a mug, and a two-piece breakfast set.

*E*nglish Drape

This very attractive vase with a gilded top stands 9¾" tall and has a base diameter of nearly 2". It is thin glass and looks much like opalescent products from England so I've taken liberty with the name. If anyone has additional information on this pattern, I'd appreciate hearing about it. I would suspect white and blue examples were also made.

*E*nglish Duck

Slightly larger than the American Little Swan pieces from Northwood, Dugan, and Fenton, this one is marked RD #31844, indicating it was made in England in 1885. We believe it may be from Sowerby but we could be wrong. At any rate, we truly thank Jon Coppenbarger for sharing this beauty with us.

Ellen

Elson Dew Drop

English Drape

English Duck

English Salt Dip

Estate

Everglades

*E*nglish Salt Dip

What a fancy piece of table service this is! The vaseline opalescent salt dip, measuring 2¼" wide and 1⅜" tall, sits atop a silver tray that bears the marking: JH EPNS. The coloring of the dip (or fill) is typically English but we're confident these came in other colors too. There is no RD number on the piece shown.

*E*state

Also called Stippled Estate, this pattern is known to have been made by the Dugan/Diamond Company in 1906 and by Model Flint in the 1900 – 1902 years. In opalescent glass, colors are white, blue, or green, but it is also found in carnival glass and in green, amber, and speckled glass. Vases are of three sizes (2½", 3½", 5½") and Model Flint also made a cruet shape.

*E*verglades

Originally called Carnelian, this Northwood pattern dates from 1903. It was made in several treatments beside opalescent glass including custard and purple slag. Opalescent colors are white, blue, and canary, with some limited production in green. Shapes made are table sets, water sets, oval berry sets, cruets, salt shakers, and jelly compotes.

*Everglades
(Cambridge)*

Everglades (Cambridge)

Everglades is a production name used by the Cambridge Company covering a line of items made from 1920 to the 1930s. The compote shown in white opalescent glass is simply one design from this line. It measures 7½" in diameter. In 1933, the Cambridge catalog listed 43 items in this line called Everglades, including vases with flower patterns, and a bowl with an Indian on horseback hunting buffalo. The line was made in many treatments and colors from 1924 to 1958.

Fan

Long considered a Northwood pattern, Fan is actually from the Dugan/Diamond plant, shown in a 1907 company ad in water sets, berry sets, and table sets in ivory (custard), and opalescent glass in colors of green, white, and blue. In a whimsey plate that was shaped from the spooner, the glass almost glows with opalescence. Fan was also made in emerald green and cobalt blue, sometimes with gold decoration, as well as, limited shapes in carnival glass.

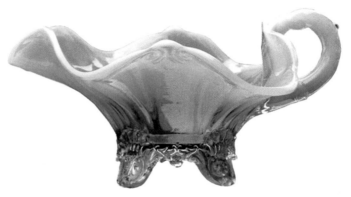

Fan

Fancy Fantails

While others credit this pattern to the Northwood Company, I'm convinced it is from Jefferson. As I've said before, research has convinced me most, if not all, of the cranberry decorated items came from Jefferson Glass. Fancy Fantails dates from 1905 and can be found in both rose bowls and candy dishes from the same mould. Colors are white, blue, green, and vaseline.

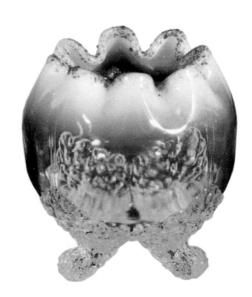

Fancy Fantails

Feathers

*Fenton's #100
(Ringed Bowl)*

Fenton's #220 Stripe

*F*eathers

No question about the maker of this vase since most are marked with the Northwood trademark. Vases are the only shape, and the colors are white, blue, and green opalescent, as well as carnival glass colors. Sizes range from 7" to a pulled 13". I've seen a blue opalescent and a white opalescent vase with gold edging.

*F*enton's #100 (Ringed Bowl)

Made first in 1929, this small bowl on stubby feet measures 7½" across and the plate from the same mould is ½" wider. Colors in opalescent glass are amethyst and vaseline, but I suspect others were made. The only pattern is the exterior rings that extend from the feet up the sides of the piece.

*F*enton's #220 Stripe

Found in iced tea sets (both pitcher and tumblers have contrasting colored handles) and nights sets (tumble-ups), this was a popular Fenton pattern, produced in 1929. Colors are blue, green, white, and vaseline, and there are two shapes and sizes in pitchers. Note that the one shown has a matching lid but not all shapes do.

Fenton's #260

Fenton's #260

This regal 7" tall compote was made by the Fenton Art Glass Company in all sorts of glass treatments that include ebony opaque, stretch glass, Grecian gold carnival, and opalescent glass as shown, where the colors are white, topaz, or blue. Production of the compote dates from 1915 to the 1930s in ruby glass.

Fenton's #370

This beauty dates from the 1924 – 1927 period of Fenton production. The cameo opalescent coloring is a real treat and I'm happy to be able to show this example. This same coloring can be found in many patterns and shapes in the Fenton line including bowls, vases, nappies, and bon-bons. The base color of the glass is a strong amber and the opalescence is a rich creamy tint.

Fenton's Vintage (Leaf)

Seen mostly in carnival glass, this very distinct Fenton pattern dates from 1909 – 1910 and can be recognized by its large leaf center as well as the five bunches of grapes that are grouped around the bowl. The exterior is plain, as is the marie. Colors reported are white, blue, and a rare amethyst. All colors are hard to find and well worth the search.

Fenton's #370

Fenton's Vintage

Fern

Finecut and Roses

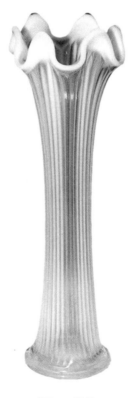

*Fine Rib
(Fenton)*

*F*ern

From several makers including West Virginia Glass, Beaumont Glass, Model Flint Glass, and possibly Northwood, this pattern is much like Daisy and Fern without the daisy. Shapes are water sets, cruets, salt shakers, syrups, sugar shakers, toothpick holders, a covered butterdish, a covered sugar, a creamer, a spooner, berry sets, a celery vase, a finger bowl, a mustard pot, and a bitters bottle. Colors are white, blue, and cranberry opalescent. It dates from 1898 to 1906 depending on the maker. Fenton has also reproduced this pattern in the 1950s.

*F*inecut and Roses

Early opalescent production of this pattern was at Jefferson's Steubenville plant, however Northwood later produced this pattern in their lines of custard and carnival glass. Colors in opalescent glass are white, blue, and green. Shapes (all from the same mould) are footed candy dishes, rose bowls, and a shape called a spooner that is slightly ruffled.

*F*ine Rib (Fenton)

We're very happy to be the first to show this very rare Fenton vase pattern in opalescent glass. Until now, the Fine Rib vase was well known in carnival glass and scarce in plain colored pieces such as ice green and pink. But as you can see, the pattern was made in a beautiful vaseline opalescent treatment. This vase stands 11^{1}/$_{3}$" tall with a 2^{7}/$_{8}$" base and a 3^{5}/$_{8}$" top opening. The opalescence runs well down the ribs and is just stunning! I believe this vase was made in the 1908 – 1910 era and there may well be white, blue, and green examples that exist. We are in the debt of Craig and Brenda Kuckelburg for sharing this rare find.

*F*ish-in-the-Sea

There is a good bit of doubt about the origin of this very strong pattern but both Northwood and Dugan/Diamond are strong possibilities. It has been found with some goofus decoration which both companies used, but it has a European look. Colors are white, blue, and green. This vase is a scarce item, much sought by collectors.

*F*ishnet Epergne

Known primarily as a carnival glass pattern with a dome-based bowl that held the fishnet lily, this Dugan/Diamond pattern was also made in opalescent glass where the lily can be found both in the bowl or sold with a decorative metal holder. Production was in the 1911 – 1912 era and colors found are white, blue, and perhaps green opalescent glass. Shown is a single metal all-purpose holder with the Fishnet lily.

*F*ishscale and Beads

Usually found in carnival glass, this Dugan/Diamond pattern is a rather scarce item in opalescent glass. The "fishscales" are on the interior and the string of beading on the outside. Colors are mostly white or blue, but I certainly wouldn't rule out vaseline or green. If you look closely, you will see a close resemblance to the Blocked Thumbprint & Beads pattern, also made by Dugan/Diamond. The same mould exterior was used for both. This piece is shown with the granite finish.

Fish-in-the-Sea

Fishnet Epergne

Fishscale and Beads

Flora

Floral Eyelet

Fluted Bars and Beads

Flora

Dating from 1898, this Beaumont pattern can be found in a host of shapes including table sets, water sets, berry sets, shakers, cruets, syrups, toothpick holders, compotes, celery vases, and several bowl novelty shapes. Colors are blue, white, and vaseline with some items gilded. Other types of glass were also made in Flora including crystal and emerald green, which can also be found with gilding.

Floral Eyelet

Little is known about this very scarce pattern; it is believed to be a product of Northwood/National or even Dugan at the Indiana, Pennsylvania, plant. The time of production has been speculated from 1896 to 1905 with the only shapes being a water pitcher and tumbler in white, blue, and cranberry opalescent; the tumbler is shown here. The reproduced pitcher, made by the L. G. Wright Company, is shown on page 166 of our previous book. The new pitchers have reeded handles while the old do not.

Fluted Bars and Beads

While previous writers have credited this very interesting pattern to the Northwood Company, I am convinced it is a Jefferson Glass Company product, dating to 1905 or 1906. The colors in opalescent glass are white, blue, green, and vaseline, often with a cranberry edging (a reason to suggest Jefferson as the maker). The design is a simple one of two sections of threading and beads that border a center area of fluting.

Fluted Scrolls (Jackson)

Made by Northwood in 1898 under the name "Klondyke," this pattern is known today as Fluted Scrolls or Jackson. It can be found in crystal, custard, green clear glass, or opalescent glass in white, blue, or vaseline. Shapes include a table set, water set, berry set, cruet, shakers, puff box (also known as a baby butter dish), one-lily epergne, and various novelty bowl shapes. When enamel decorated, this pattern is sometimes called Fluted Scrolls with Flower Band.

Fluted Scrolls (Jackson)

Fluted Scrolls with Vine

Shown as early as 1899 in a Butler Brothers ad, this Northwood Glass Company pattern is one of my favorite vase designs. It is known in white, blue, and canary and may also show up in green one of these days. I am continually amazed at the colors and patterns that have been overlooked for years. The design of flowers, stems, and leaves winding around a fluted, cone-shaped vase is very pretty; when you add the base of spread leaves and the top rim of scalloped blossoms, the whole piece becomes a real work of art.

*Fluted Scrolls
with Vine*

Forked Stripe

If you look at the base of this barber bottle, you'll see the stripes end in points so I've given it this name. This piece is white opalescent, measures 7" tall, and has a base diameter of 3½". It is marked on the base "PAT-PENDING." The maker isn't known at this time, but a pitcher from a very limited Imperial Glass production in 1930 has this same pointed finish to its stripe except it is reversed and faces upward. Other colors probably exist, but I can't be sure.

Forked Stripe

Four-Footed Hobnail

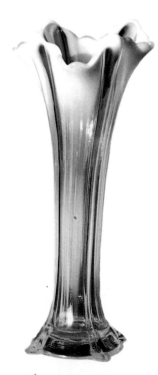

Four Pillars

Frosted Leaf and
Basketweave

*F*our-Footed Hobnail

After we showed this pattern in the last edition of this book, we were informed this pattern was a product of LaBelle Glass of Bridgeport, Ohio, in 1886. Only the table set pieces are known, all with peg feet. In opalescent glass, colors are dark blue, white, and canary, but the pattern was also made in crystal, vaseline, and blue glass.

*F*our Pillars

Made in opalescent glass by Northwood and later in carnival glass by both Northwood and Dugan/Diamond, this vase is also found with advertising on some Northwood carnival pieces. Opalescent colors are white, blue, green, and vaseline (shown). The four columns or pillars run from top to bottom and end in four rounded feet. Ranging in size from 9" to 14" tall, some pieces from Dugan/Diamond have gilding.

*F*rosted Leaf and Basketweave

Credited to Northwood, this pattern seems to be found only in the table set pieces. It dates to 1905 and the colors known are blue, vaseline, and white opalescent, as well as crystal. Interestingly enough, the exterior pattern of the famous Rose Show bowls match this pattern exactly without the leaf, and I suspect the spooner mould was retooled to make this fine bowl exterior.

Garland of Roses

Garland of Roses

Found primarily in crystal or vaseline glass, this is a small cake stand or card tray, flattened from a jelly compote shape. It is the first piece of opalescent glass we've heard about in this pattern and since all the crystal pieces are considered rare, this piece has to be ultra-rare. We'd like to hear from anyone having other shapes or colors of this pattern in an opalescent treatment. The piece shown measures 6⅝" across and stands 2" tall.

Gonterman (Adonis) Hob

Like the Swirl pattern with the same titles, this is an Aetna Glass pattern dating to 1886 (despite bearing "Pat'd Aug 4, 1876" on the base). Unlike the Swirl pattern, there doesn't seem to be a blue version, only the amber. Needless to say, since only the cruet shown has been reported, it is extremely hard to find and has to be considered rare.

*Gonterman
(Adonis) Hob*

Gonterman Swirl

Found on both frosted and opalescent pieces, this pattern is attributed to Aetna Glass by most collectors (the patent was issued to Hobbs, Brockunier & Company for the joining process). One writer believes Hobbs may have licensed Aetna to do the pattern. At any rate, pieces are known in either blue or amber with opalescence in table sets, water sets (rare), berry sets, cruet, syrup, celery vase, lamp shade, and a toothpick holder (sometimes in a metal frame). Pieces are marked "Patented August 4, 1876" but this refers to the joining process and not a production date, which is a decade later.

Gonterman Swirl

Gossamer Threads

Grape and Cable

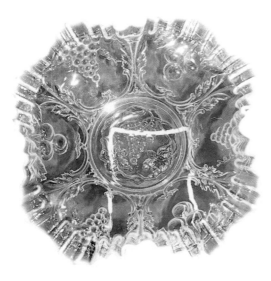

Grape and Cherry

Gossamer Threads

Mould blown, this hand decorated finger bowl has been seen in a ruffled bowl and a matching 6½" plate all in blue with the cranberry threading. The glass is light and very thin and the example shown measures 4" wide and 2½" tall. I have a strong feeling this glass may be European, but it is, without question, quality all the way.

Grape and Cable

Very little production of this pattern in opalescent glass is found besides the rare bon-bon in the last edition and several shapings of this large footed fruit bowl (some are turned like a centerpiece bowl). The bon-bon has been reported in vaseline only while the footed bowl has been seen in white, vaseline, and is suspected in blue. The bon-bon may have been made in white also and carries the famous Northwood basketweave as the exterior pattern. In addition, the Fenton Company made a Grape and Cable large fruit bowl nearly identical to Northwood's; it is found in white opalescent also.

Grape and Cherry

Known in both carnival glass and opalescent glass, the first production was by Sowerby of England, but blue opalescent has been reproduced by L. G. Wright as simply "Cherry." Old opalescent pieces are known in white, blue, and canary, and these, of course, came from Sowerby. Several shapes can be found that include deep round bowls, ruffled square bowls, and oval banana bowls, all from the same mould. Reproduced for L. G. Wright in 1978.

Grape and Vine

Grape and Vine

I haven't been able to learn a thing about this very pretty pattern, but the owner calls it Grape and Vine so I'll stick with that name until I learn differently. It reminds one of Panelled Grape but on close examination it isn't the same at all. The Jack-in-the-Pulpit shape makes it special, and I'm sure it came in other colors.

Grapevine Cluster

Made by the Northwood Glass Company in 1905, this very realistic vase pattern is found in white, blue, aqua, canary, and green (rare) opalescent glass as well as a treatment of purple slag the company called "Mosaic." The design features heavy grape and leaf patterns, grapevine supporting branches, and a grape leaf base. The pattern is a collector's favorite and always brings a high price when sold. Some of the blue examples tend toward a soft aqua color.

Grapevine Cluster

Grecian Urn

The owner of this small pretty vase (4¼" tall with a 2" base diameter) named this piece and it seems to fit. I believe this piece may be English, but I could be wrong. The opalescence is outstanding. I'd be interested in hearing from anyone who knows more about this pattern or can tell me of other colors.

Grecian Urn

Greek Key and Ribs

Greek Key and Scales

Harrow

Greek Key and Ribs

This Northwood bowl pattern is similar to the Greek Key and Scales bowl shown below. Dating from the 1907 production, the dome-based bowl can be found in white, blue, green, and canary, as well as the host of carnival colors. Just why one company would create two moulds so similar is a mystery, but it seemed to happen frequently, especially in opalescent and carnival glass. Perhaps competition forced so many variations, but I can't be sure. At any rate, it makes collecting more interesting for all of us.

Greek Key and Scales

Made by the Northwood Company in 1905, this often marked pattern is well-known in both opalescent glass and carnival. The bowl shape has a dome base and is usually ruffled. Opalescent colors are white, green, and blue.

Harrow

This English pattern has been unnamed to the best of my knowledge so I've taken the liberty of calling it Harrow. It stands 6" tall and bears an RD #217749. It was probably made in table set pieces, and a stemmed wine or cordial has been seen. Colors besides blue probably include white and canary.

Heart Handled Open O's

Heart Handled Open O's

While this is primarily the same pattern as the Open O's we show on page 99, the handled ring basket has always been shown on its own and we will keep it that way. It is a Northwood pattern, 1905 – 1906. Colors are white, blue, and green, with canary a strong possibility.

Hearts and Clubs

This Jefferson Glass Company pattern was originally their #274 and was produced about 1905. As you can see, the footed bowl shown here has a goofus treatment, but it can be found on blue and green opalescent glass as well. The three feet of the bowl are shaped like those on the Daisy and Plume pieces made by Northwood and later Dugan, but are solid without any portholes.

Hearts and Flowers

This well-known Northwood pattern can be found in carnival, custard, and opalescent glass. In the latter, it is seen on compotes and bowls in white, blue, and very rarely vaseline. Production dates from 1908, when the maker added several well-known patterns to their opalescent production on a limited basis, including Singing Birds, Peacock on the Fence, Rose Show, Grape and Cable, Three Fruits, Bushel Basket, Acorn Burrs, Beaded Cable, Finecut and Roses, and Daisy and Plume. All were made mainly in white or blue, with a few vaseline items.

Hearts and Clubs

Hearts and Flowers

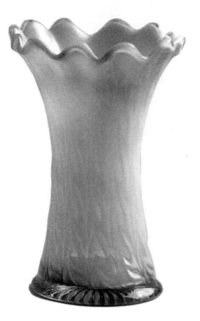

Heatherbloom

Heron and Peacock

Herringbone (Plain)

Heatherbloom

From Jefferson Glass circa 1905 and called their #268, this seldom discussed pattern is found only on vases. Colors in opalescent glass are the usual white, blue, and green with the latter hardest to find. The design has a tendency to blur as the vase is swung to taller sizes, and only the shorter ones really show the pattern at its best.

Heron and Peacock

While I have very little information about this child's mug known as Heron and Peacock, I believe it is an old example. I've been told it has been made in many glass treatments over the years and is listed in one book on children's collectibles as having once been made in crystal and cobalt blue, but this is the first I've actually seen. It may well have been made in other opalescent colors, and a blue or canary one would be outstanding. The design has a peacock on one side and the heron on the other with floral sprays dividing them. The opalescence is quite good. It is currently being reproduced by Boyd Crystal Art Glass, Cambridge, Ohio.

Herringbone (Plain)

Since shards of this pattern were found at the Indiana, Pennsylvania, plant, we can be confident one of the makers of Herringbone (both plain and ribbed) was the Northwood Glass Company. Shard colors were white, yellow, and blue, but of course, cranberry items are also known. Items known are water sets, cruets, syrups, and crimped salad bowls. Some treatments are cased mother-of-pearl in a satin finish. The plain Herringbone dates to 1885, when Harry Northwood was at the Phoenix Glass concern.

Herringbone (Ribbed)

*H*erringbone (Ribbed)

As I said in the narrative about plain Herringbone, this is most likely a Northwood pattern, found on water sets, cruets, syrups, and crimped salad bowls in white, blue, cranberry, and canary opalescent glass. While the plain Herringbone came first and dates to Northwood's days at Phoenix, the ribbed Herringbone is believed to date to about 1902, at the Indiana plant. Since I felt the two treatments were so different, I chose to discuss them as separate items.

*H*illtop Vines

This unusual compote is shown in Northwood ads as early as 1906, so we know who made it. It can be found in white, blue, and green opalescent glass and stands roughly 5" tall. Outstanding features are the leaves that overlap, making up the bowl of the compote, the branch-like legs that form the stem, and the domed base covered with tiny bubble-like circles.

Hilltop Vines

*H*obnail (Hobbs)

Here is the Hobnail from Hobbs, Brockunier. Shapes made in this well-known pattern are water sets, table sets, berry sets (square shaped), cruets, shaker, syrups, finger bowls, celery vase, barber bottle, water tray, bride's basket with frame, and five sizes of pitchers. Production of the Hobbs Hobnail design began in 1885 and lasted until 1892. Colors reported are white, blue, rubina, vaseline, and cranberry.

Hobnail (Hobbs)

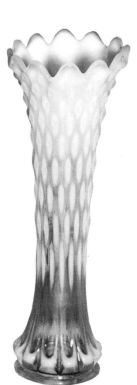

*Hobnail and
Paneled
Thumbprint*

Hobnail-in-Square

Holly and Berry

Hobnail and Paneled Thumbprint

Most collectors credit this pattern to Northwood but I know of no proof it was made at that concern. The pattern dates to 1905 or 1906 and can be found in berry sets, table sets, water sets, and vases that have been pulled from the spooner shape. Colors are white, blue, or canary in opalescent glass. It is a shame no toothpick holder, cruet, or salt shakers are known.

Hobnail-in-Square

Made by the Aetna Glass and Mfg. Company of Bellaire, Ohio, this pattern dates from 1887 and is often confused with a recent pattern called Vesta made by the Fenton Company since the 1950s. Colors for the original pattern are primarily white but it was also made in crystal. Shapes are water sets, table sets, berry sets, a celery vase, salt shakers, and compotes.

Holly and Berry

Primarily a carnival glass pattern from Dugan/Diamond, the nappy shape has surfaced in opalescent glass in white only (surely blue and green were also made). The design is a good one with a center cluster of holly berries and leaves and the same design in a wreath shape around the rim with three strings of leaves and berries. The nappy is a large one, measuring 7" across the top, from handle to pouring lip.

Honeycomb

*H*oneycomb

Called Opal Honeycomb by some collectors, this design is also known as Hobbs Honeycomb but we have no proof it was made at the Hobbs, Brockunier factory. It is found in a 7" bowl as well as the vase shape, all from the same mould. Besides the honeycombing which is stretched out of shape in the vase shape, there is a very nice ribbed skirting to the base.

*H*oneycomb and Clover

Made by the Fenton Company in several types of glass including carnival, opalescent, and gilt decorated. Production in opalescent glass dates from 1910, and the colors known are the usual white, blue, and green. However, amethyst is a definite possibility and would be a real find. The pattern is exterior and consists of an all-over honeycombing with clover and leaves twining over it. Shapes in opalescent glass are water sets, berry sets, table sets, and novelty bowls.

Honeycomb and Clover

*I*dyll

Made by Jefferson Glass, Idyll can be found in water sets, table sets, berry sets, a toothpick holder, cruet and salt shakers sometimes grouped on a tray, and an intermediate size bowl. Colors in opalescent glass are blue, green, and white, and the pattern can also be found in crystal, gilded green, and blue. Idyll dates from 1907.

Idyll

Inside Ribbing

Intaglio

Interior Flute

Inside Ribbing

Beaumont Glass of Martins Ferry, Ohio, made this very pretty glass in the early 1900s, and while it isn't plentiful, many times it is overlooked. Colors are white, canary, blue, and possibly green; the shapes are berry sets, table sets, water sets, toothpick holders, a cruet, a syrup, salt shakers, a cruet set, and a celery vase. Some pieces have enameled decoration adding to the interest.

Intaglio

One of Northwood's earlier patterns dating from 1897 in custard production, Intaglio was made in a host of shapes including table sets, water sets, berry sets, a cruet, salt shakers, a jelly compote, and many novelty shapes. Colors made in opalescent glass are white, blue, and occasionally canary, but other treatments such as gilded emerald green and, of course, custard are available.

Interior Flute

Not to be confused with Fenton's Interior Panel pattern, this one has wide panels that are about twice as far apart as the latter. Shown is a 5½" vase in lavender opalescent glass with a jack-in-the-pulpit top. We believe this is a Dugan/ Diamond pattern but can't be sure at this time. It probably came in blue, white, and green opalescent glass as well.

Interior Panel

Interior Panel

This very nice Fenton vase dates from the early 1920s and besides the fine example in amber opalescent, I've seen it in Cameo opalescent, iridized stretch glass in Celeste Blue, Velva Rose, and Florentine Green, all from the 1921 – 1927 era of production. The same mould was used to make a trumpet vase also. The example shown is 8" tall and has a fan spread of 5".

Interior Poinsettia (Pressed)

Unlike the blown poinsettia pattern, this one is pressed and seems to be found only on the tumbler shape. It is known in carnival glass in marigold only, on clear glass, and opalescent glass in blue, green, or white. The pattern is credited to the Northwood Company, and a trademark is on the inside of the tumbler.

Interior Swirl

Much like the Inside Ribbing pattern but with a twist, this very pretty rose bowl is perfectly plain on the outside and has a ribbing that has been twisted on the interior. Notice the cranberry frit along the top indicating this pattern is most likely from Jefferson Glass. One writer dates this pattern to the 1890s, but I'd place it closer to 1904 or 1905. The canary coloring is quite good and the base prominent.

Interior Poinsettia

Interior Swirl

Inverted
Chevron

Inverted Fan and Feather

Iris with Meander

Jackson

Inverted Chevron

When I first saw this very attractive vase, I thought it was Plume Panels, a pattern well-known to carnival glass collectors. But on close examination, it is very different. I suspect it may be from Jefferson Glass and I've named it Inverted Chevron. While blue and green are the only colors I've seen, I'm sure it must have come in white.

Inverted Fan and Feather

First made by Northwood in other treatments including custard glass (Dugan/Diamond made the opalescent items), Inverted Fan and Feather can be found in water sets, table sets, berry sets, a jelly compote, punch sets, a toothpick holder, a salt shaker, a rare cruet, and many whimsies that include spittoons and rosebowls. Opalescent colors are white, blue, green (rare), and canary, and Dugan also made a few items in carnival glass.

Iris with Meander

Iris with Meander is also known as Fleur-de-Lis Scrolled and is a product of Jefferson Glass, dating to 1902 or 1903. It was made in table sets, water sets, berry sets (two sizes of sauces), toothpick holder, salt shaker, jelly compote, vase, pickle dish, and the plate shown. Colors are flint, blue, canary, green, and rarely amber opalescent, as well as crystal, blue, green, and amethyst glass with decoration.

Jackson

May I say I personally hate not calling this pattern and Fluted Scrolls by the original name that covered both patterns, Klondyke, but I will bow to previous writers. Jackson is a Northwood pattern and can be found on table sets, water sets, berry sets, cruets, candy dishes, and a mini-epergne. Colors are white, blue, canary, and limited amounts of green. It was also made in custard glass.

Jazz

While I can't find this pattern pictured in any Dugan/Diamond ad, I feel sure it came from that company. Note the base has two levels and the unusual treatment of the top is sassy and bold, so I've named it Jazz and feel that is certainly a descriptive title. Shown in blue, it probably came in white and green also. Date of production should be in the 1906 – 1909 time frame, I'd bet. It is 6" tall.

Jefferson #270 (Jefferson Colonial)

At first glance this looks like another Jefferson pattern called Iris With Meander. Indeed, the moulds may have been the same, for this design is missing the fleur-de-lis at the base and the beading in the slots. Shown is the master berry bowl in blue, so we know the berry set was made. Colors are surely the usual Jefferson ones of white, blue, green, and canary, and I'd like to hear from anyone who has additional information about shapes and colors.

Jefferson Shield

This very rare pattern was from the Jefferson Glass Company, produced as their #262 pattern. It is a dome-based bowl, found in green, white, and blue opalescent. It has a series of 13 shields around the center of the bowl. If you are the owner of one of these bowls, consider yourself very lucky, for less than one dozen in all colors are known!

Jefferson Spool

This very unusual hyacinth vase by the Jefferson Glass Company looks as if it were turned on a lathe. It stands approximately 8" tall and was made in 1905. Colors reported in opalescent glass are white, green, blue, and vaseline. No other shapes have been seen, but it could easily have been opened into a compote.

Jazz

Jefferson #270

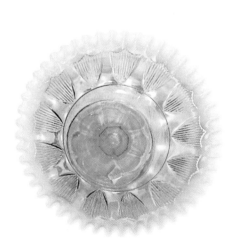

Jefferson Shield

Jefferson Spool

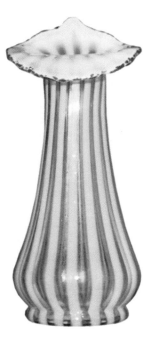

Jefferson Stripe

Jefferson Wheel

Jester Epergne

Jefferson Stripe

Shown in a 1902 Jefferson ad as their #33 Lily vase, this pretty jack-in-the-pulpit shaped vase (it is also known with a ruffled top) is 8" tall. Colors known are white opalescent, blue opalescent, and the green opalescent shown, and pieces may be found with or without the cranberry glass frit on the top edge. The green tends to be a bit dark, almost an emerald green shade.

Jefferson Wheel

This very attractive bowl dating from 1905 is, as the name implies, another pattern from Jefferson Glass. It was originally Jefferson's #260 pattern and can be found in white, blue, or green opalescent glass. It has been reported in carnival, but I seriously doubt that possibility.

Jester Epergne

The name for this 9" one-lily epergne comes from the figure on the metal base and actually the lily from Single Lily Spool or others could be used in this holder. Shown is a very nice green opalescent one with tight J.I.P. crimping. It surely came in white, blue, and vaseline, too.

Jewel and Fan

Jewel and Fan

Jefferson made a lot of opalescent glass and here is still another pattern which was originally identified as their #125. It is found on bowls and an elongated banana bowl in white, blue, green, and rarely canary. The design is simple but very effective.

Jewel and Flower

Made by the Northwood Company in 1904, and originally called Encore, this very attractive pattern can be found on water sets, table sets, berry sets, cruets, and salt shakers. Colors are white, blue, and canary, often decorated with gilding as in the example shown. Incidentally, there is a variant with the design going all the way to the base and eliminating the beading and threading band.

Jewel and Flower

Jewelled Heart

Long credited to Northwood, Jewelled Heart (or Victor, as it was originally called) was first made by Dugan in 1905. Shapes available are table sets, water sets, berry sets, a syrup, sugar shaker, a condiment set consisting of cruet, salt and pepper shakers, and toothpick holder on a round flat tray or plate. Colors in opalescent glass are white, green, and blue, but the pattern is also found in carnival glass, crystal, green, and blue decorated glass, and very rarely ivory or custard glass. Some items are marked with the Diamond-D marking.

Jewelled Heart

*Jewels and
Drapery*

Jolly Bear

Keyhole

Jewels and Drapery

This very pretty Northwood vase dates to 1907 and can be found in ads from that year. As you can see, the drapery is very well done with a tiny tassel ending between the folds. Around the base is a series of jewels or raised dots. Strangely, in a Northwood ad in a 1906 Lyons Brothers catalog, there is a similar vase shown that has an additional row of pendants below the jewels. The ad is labeled the Fairmont opal assortment. To date I haven't seen any examples of this vase.

Jolly Bear

Made by the Jefferson Glass Company in 1906 or 1907 and found in opalescent glass in white, blue or green. The white pieces sometimes have gilding on them, leading to the possibility they were also used with a goofus treatment. Shapes are round, ruffled, or ever tri-cornered. The bear is very much like that on the U.S. Glass pattern called Frolicking Bears and would be an excellent companion piece.

Keyhole

Also shown in 1905 Dugan Glass Company ads is the Keyhole pattern. It can be found in opalescent glass on bowls that have a dome base in white, blue, and green; and painted or goofus treatment on the white. A few years later, it was adapted for use as the exterior of carnival glass bowls with Raindrop pattern as an interior and on a very rare marigold bowl where the exterior is plain and Keyhole became the interior pattern.

King Richard

King Richard

The owner of this very attractive compote named it, and I have no argument with the name since I haven't been able to find it listed anywhere. It appears to be a British pattern, with an unusual stem of scrolled supports. The interior has an equally appealing pattern of swirling branches and leaves as well as a file shield with scroll edging. If anyone knows more about this pattern, I'd certainly like to hear from them. The compote is 4" tall, 6¾" wide, and has a 2⅝" base.

Kittens

From the Fenton Company (their #299) and primarily found in carnival glass; rare cups and saucers are known in crystal, royal blue, and these two items in amethyst opalescent glass that date to 1908 production. The saucer is really a 4" plate since all Kittens pieces were toy items, intended for children. Probably other pieces in this opalescent treatment were made but none have been reported.

Kittens

Lady Caroline

Made in 1891 by Davidson, this English pattern was first produced in blue as their patented Blue Pearline, but as you can see, it was also made in canary or vaseline opalescent. Shapes found are a creamer and open sugar (#225 in their ads), baskets (their #240 and #242), a two-handled spill or vase, and several novelty shapes, most with three handles like the whimsey shape shown.

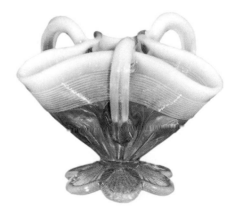

Lady Caroline

Late Coinspot

Lattice and Daisy

Lattice and Points

*L*ate Coinspot

Here is a Fenton version of the famed Coinspot. This one dating from the 1925 – 1929 era was called an iced tea set in advertising and had a taller tumbler with it. Colors were white, blue, and green. As you can easily see, it has a semi-cannonball shape and the handle is rather thick. In 1931 Fenton made this same pitcher with a dark, contrasting handle, and teamed it with mugs with the same handle treatment.

*L*attice and Daisy

Shown in a Butler Brothers ad in 1914 that features several Dugan Glass patterns in opalescent glass, the Lattice and Daisy tumbler was apparently the only shape in this pattern offered in this type of glass. In carnival glass, the complete water set, as well as a berry set, is shown. The opalescent colors listed in the ad for this tumbler were white and blue, but as you can see, a very rare vaseline was made. Strangely, the iridized glass production of this pattern was also 1914, so it may just be that the opalescent pieces were made to fill the packing amounts needed for shipment, since all items in the opalescent ad are considered quite scarce. They include the Mary Ann vase, the Windflower bowl, the Stork and Rushes mug, the Constellation compote, and Fishscale and Beads items.

*L*attice and Points

This Dugan pattern is pulled from the same mould that produced the Vining Twigs plates and bowls that were made in carnival glass as well as the vases. In opalescent glass, the vases are usually short and haven't been pulled or swung as most vases are. Colors are white, mostly, but scarce blue examples are known and I suspect green was made also. Production of the opalescent pieces dates from 1907.

Lattice Medallions

This very graceful pattern is from the Northwood Company and is sometimes marked with the famous "N." Found primarily in bowl shapes, often very ruffled and ornately shaped, Lattice Medallions can be found in the usual opalescent colors of white, blue, and green. Shown is a very pretty white opalescent bowl with the tri-corner shaping.

Laura (Single Flower Framed)

Here is another example of poor naming; the Laura name is from Rose Presznick but the pattern has long been called Single Flower Framed by carnival glass collectors. It is a Dugan pattern, found only on the exterior of nappies, bowls, and this very rare ruffled plate. Colors previously reported are white and blue opalescent, as well as carnival colors (especially peach opalescent). These scarce items date from the 1909 period of Dugan production.

Laurel Swag and Bows

While I've searched every reference I could find about this pattern, it doesn't seem to be shown anywhere. We know it was made by the Fenton Company about 1908, for they made the only amethyst opalescent glass around that time. As you can see, there are laurel swags tied with a ribbon and bow, as well as cosmos-like flowers and an unusual bull's-eye with a swirl of connecting leaves. I would appreciate any information about this pretty gas shade.

Lattice Medallions

Laura

Laurel Swag and Bows

Leaf and Beads

Leaf and Diamonds

Leaf and Leaflets

Leaf and Beads

Just why Northwood made two variant treatments to this pattern is unclear, but both are shown here. One has twig feet and a few changes in leaves while the other has a dome base. The latter should be called a variant. Production of the twig-footed bowl began in 1905, but by 1906 both styles were being advertised. Colors are blue, white, and green opalescent plus custard glass and carnival pieces.

Leaf and Diamonds

I apologize for calling this a Dugan/Diamond pattern in the last edition of this book. It is shown in a 1908 Butler Brothers ad with other items that were made by the Jefferson Glass Company! Found in white, blue, and a scarce green in opalescent glass, this design could be a companion pattern to Jefferson's Hearts and Clubs pattern. Leaf and Diamonds has three large spatula feet.

Leaf and Leaflets

Here is another of those patterns that appeared first in Northwood's lineup (1907 ads) and later became part of the Dugan production line. The opalescent examples in blue, white, and goofus are Northwood, however the same mould turns up later as a Dugan carnival glass pattern called Long Leaf in a beautiful peach opalescent iridized bowl. In addition, Long Leaf can be found as the exterior design for bowls and baskets of the Stippled Petals design in peach opalescent, also made by Dugan!

Leaf Chalice

Leaf Chalice

Made by Northwood while a part of the National combine, Leaf Chalice appears in a May 1903 Butler Brothers ad that featured three shapings of the piece. Colors usually found are white or blue, but green was also made, as you can see, and is considered a rare color in this pattern.

Leaf Rosette and Beads

Made by the Dugan/Diamond Company beginning in 1906, this pattern seems to be a cousin to Blocked Thumbprint and Beads with the addition of the chain of leaves added. And if you take a look at the Single Poinsettia pattern, you will see just how similar these patterns are. Leaf Rosette and Beads is a scarce pattern and was most likely made in the usual colors, but the only ones I've seen are white and green.

Leaf Rosette and Beads

Lily Pool Epergne

While we can't be sure of the maker of this one-lily piece, the design of the bowl and the general shape of the lily lead us to believe this may be an unmarked Northwood pattern. If so, it was probably made in white as well as blue opalescent glass. It is all one piece, a remarkable mould feat to say the least.

Lily Pool Epergne

Lined Heart

Linking Rings

*Lion Store Souvenir
(Beaded Stars Advertising)*

*L*ined Heart
Dating from 1906, this Jefferson Glass Company vase pattern can be found in white, blue, and green opalescent glass. The examples shown haven't been swung as many are and are about 7" tall; some range to 14".

*L*inking Rings
From Davidson in 1894 as their #237038 design, most pieces bear this Rd number. Shapes in opalescent glass reported are a water set, oval 8½" x 7" tray (shown), juice glass, bowls, a compote, 7½" plate, 3" creamer, and an open sugar. Colors in the opalescent treatment are a deep blue, a softer blue, and canary (vaseline).

*L*ion Store Souvenir (Beaded Stars Advertising)
Why so very few of these Fenton advertising pieces exist or why there are so very few advertising items in all of opalescent glass is a real mystery. The only pieces reported in Beaded Stars are a bowl and a plate. They read: SOUVENIR LION STORE HAMMOND and are found in blue, white, and green.

Little Nell

Despite being very plain, this vase is still a very cute item. Except for the threading above the collar base, there is no design at all and whatever the vase has going for it comes from the shaping and fine opalescence. The maker isn't certain at this time, and I'm not sure it really matters. Colors are white, blue, and green opalescent.

Little Swan (Dugan)

Slightly larger than the Northwood swan shown below, the Dugan version came along in 1909 and can be found in white, green, and blue opalescent glass and various carnival glass colors. The Fenton Company also made a version, but the breast feathering is quite different from the two versions here, more like flower petals than feathers.

Little Swan (Northwood)

Virtually the same design as the Dugan Little Swan, the Northwood version came first and is slightly smaller. It can be found in blue and white; green may be a possibility but I've only seen Dugan ones in that color. Some examples have been gilded on the head, along the rim of the opening, and down the tail.

Little Swan (Dugan)

Little Nell

Little Swan (Northwood)

Lords and Ladies

Lorna

Lotus

*L*ords and Ladies

From Davidson in England (their Rd #285312 or #285342) and found in blue or canary (vaseline) opalescent glass. Shapes include a 2¼" salt, covered butter dish, a 3" creamer, small sugar, one-handled nappy, cake plate, creamer and sugar on feet, a celery boat, platter, a 4"x6" oval bowl, and possibly a water set. The date of manufacture is October 2, 1896.

*L*orna

This should be called the traveling vase since it was first made at Model Flint in 1900, then at Northwood as their #562 the same year, then by Dugan/Diamond when Northwood left the plant, and finally by West Virginia Glass! It only seems to be a blown vase with the top whimsied. Most stand about 6½" – 7" tall and can be found in white, canary, or blue opalescent.

*L*otus

Also called Lotus Blossom by some collectors, this Albany Glass pattern is found only in the shape shown, a rose bowl shape with an attached underplate. It was made in 1900 – 1902 in white, canary, and blue opalescent glass as well as opaque glass colors of blue, green, white, or yellow. Speculation is this was made by Model Flint during their last years at Albany.

Lustre Flute

*L*ustre Flute

Also called Waffle Band or English Hob Band, this Northwood pattern is found sparingly in carnival glass, decorated glass. The opalescent colors reported are white or blue. Opalescent production began in 1907, and shapes include a water set, table set, berry set, a custard cup, and a vase shape. The pattern is a bit on the plain side and certainly not one of the better remembered ones from this company.

*M*any Loops

Made by the Jefferson Glass Company as their #247 pattern and confined to novelty bowls, rose bowls, and banana bowl shapes all from the same mould, this spirograph-like pattern of overlapping loops bordered by zig-zag threading is a distinctive design. It is found in crystal, and opalescent colors of white, blue, or green.

*M*any Ribs

This very distinctive vase with a columnal base was made by the Model Flint Glass Company of Albany, Indiana, in 1902. It can be found in white, blue, and the very attractive canary. This particular vase measures nearly 8" and has the typical slightly flared top.

Many Loops

Many Ribs

Maple Leaf

Maple Leaf Chalice

*Markham Swirl Band
with Opal Cobweb*

*M*aple Leaf

Apparently first a Northwood pattern (at least in custard glass), the opalescent items and later carnival glass production were definitely Dugan products. The opalescent glass dates from 1908 – 1910. Colors in this glass are green (scarce), white, and blue with a very rare example in vaseline. The only shape reported in opalescent glass seems to be the jelly compote, but others may certainly exist.

*M*aple Leaf Chalice

Another of the naturalistic pieces from the Northwood Company made in purple slag, as well as opalescent glass. This very pretty vase dates from the 1903 – 1905 era. Opalescent colors are white, blue, green, and vaseline. The design is much like Leaf Chalice, also from Northwood, and the two are often confused.

*M*arkham Swirl Band with Opal Cobweb

What a name! Actually there are other Markham Swirl designs with various opal designs in white, blue, cranberry, and possibly canary. The example shown is a finger lamp but examples in standard oil lamps are also known.

Mary Ann

*M*ary Ann

While this vase is well known to carnival glass collectors, it comes as a surprise to many who collect opalescent glass. It came from the Dugan Company and received its name from Fanny Mary Ann Dugan, sister of Thomas E.A. and Alfred Dugan. In carnival, the vase is known in an eight-scallop and ten-scallop top, and a three-handled, flat topped example called a loving cup. Carnival colors are marigold, amethyst, and a lighter lavender shade. There is also an amber glass example in satin finish. In opalescent glass, the only colors reported are white and blue, and both are considered rare.

May Basket

*M*ay Basket

Credited to the Jefferson Glass Company and shown in ads as their #87 pattern. For years some collectors thought it was a Northwood pattern since it has the same design as the Pump and Trough pieces. May Basket can be found in white, blue, green, and the scarce vaseline opalescent shown in three sizes.

*M*eander

Originally a Jefferson pattern (#233), the moulds were obtained by the Northwood Company after its move to the Wheeling location. The opalescent pieces in white, blue, and green are attributed to Jefferson, and the carnival bowls with Three Fruits Medallion as an interior pattern are strictly Northwood.

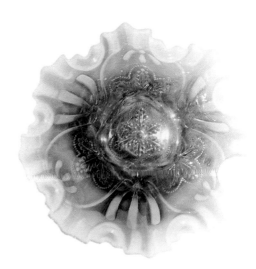

Meander

Melon Optic Swirl (Jefferson)

Melon Swirl

Milky Way

Melon Optic Swirl (Jefferson)

This very beautiful, tightly crimped bowl has a melon rib exterior that has been shaped into a swirl with cranberry edging. This bowl appears to be quite close to a series of pieces shown in a 1902 Jefferson ad, showing Stripe, Swirl, and Coin Dot items. The ad lists colors of white, blue, green, yellow (vaseline), and cranberry.

Melon Swirl

Having done a great deal of research and soul-searching, I'm convinced this very beautiful water set may well be from the Indiana, Pennsylvania, plant at the time of early Dugan production. Examples of handles just like the one on the water set shown are found in 1904 ads showing decorated sets. In addition, the enamel work is very similar to that found on several Dugan sets made between 1900 and 1905. These sets, more elaborate than most in this enameling, are consistent with Melon Swirl. I certainly hope someone out there can shed more light on this fantastic pattern. It is one of the prettiest I've ever seen.

Milky Way

Called County Kitchen by carnival collectors, this is Millersburg's only design in opalescent glass. It can be found in two sizes of bowls that are shaped in various ways including square, ruffled, or round shapes. The square bowl shown measures 4½" x 6". Milky Way is found only in white opalescent glass and was an experimental treatment the company was trying when they were forced to close.

Model Flint Reverse Swirl

First made at Buckeye Glass, this pattern was later brought to Model Flint of Albany, Indiana, where it was continued in blue, canary, and white opalescent glass. Shapes made at Albany include a 9" bowl, a table set, celery vase, a rose bowl, sugar shaker, syrup, toothpick holder, water bottle, and a vase shape. Cranberry items in this pattern were made at Buckeye Glass.

Monkey (Under a Tree)

Dating to the 1880s, this pattern found mostly in crystal, occasionally turns up in white opalescent glass. Shapes known are water sets, a finger bowl, a toothpick holder, a mug, a pickle jar, a jam jar, a celery vase, and an ashtray; not all shapes have been found in anything but crystal. Opalescent pieces are very collectible and expensive.

National's #17

Shown in National's 1901 catalog along with other patterns created by Harry Northwood. The vase is called a bouquet vase and stands 8" tall. Colors are rather dark in this opalescent piece, but green, blue, and canary are reported.

Model Flint Reverse Swirl

Monkey (Under a Tree)

National's #17

National Swirl   *Nesting Robins*

Netted Cherry

National Swirl

While I haven't seen this opalescent pattern shown in National ads, a 1900 ad from a G. Sommers and Company catalog does show a very similarly shaped pitcher in a decorated design. Please note the reed handle; the ad had three pitchers with reed handles, indicating the National designation might indeed be right. Colors listed in the catalog were crystal, blue, and green but ruby was also made and perhaps the opalescent pieces evolved from these earlier models.

Nesting Robins

In the last edition we said the bowl shown was marked "EZAN" as well as "Made in France," but we now know of a bowl in this pattern that is marked "Sabino," also a French company, making glass in the 1920s and 1930s. The quality of workmanship is quite good, and only time will tell us more about this piece. The bowl shown measures 10" across and was purchased in France.

Netted Cherry

While we have no proof, we feel confident this pattern was made by Dugan/Diamond. It is found only on bowls in crystal or opalescent glass where the colors are white or blue. Shapes include round, tri-cornered, or banana shape, but all are from the same mould. Goofus examples have been reported too.

Netted Roses

Netted Roses

Made by the Northwood Company in 1906, this bowl pattern is another of those with one name for opalescent glass and another for carnival. In carnival, the pattern is called Bullseye and Leaves and is an exterior pattern also. In opalescent glass as Netted Roses, the colors are blue, green, and white, often with a goofus treatment.

New England Pineapple

The pattern shown was originally made in the mid-1800s by either the Boston & Sandwich Glass Company or the New England Glass Company in clear crystal only. We can find no reference as to who later made this opalescent stemmed champagne piece, but it matches the older clear ones exactly. Anyone with information about this piece is urged to contact us.

Northern Star

Another Fenton pattern dating to 1908, this very nice geometric is most often found in carnival glass or crystal but can rarely be found in large plates in white, blue, or green opalescent glass. Just why the small bowls and plates were not made in opalescent treatment is a mystery since 5" bowls, 7" plates, and 11" plates are all known in crystal.

*New England
Pineapple*

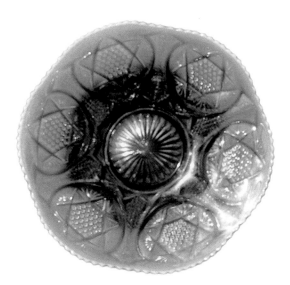

Northern Star

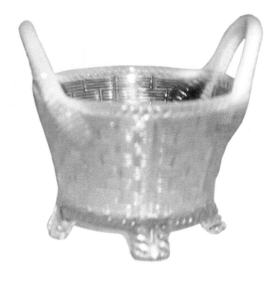

Northwood (Bushel) Basket

Northwood Block

*Northwood's
Many Ribs*

Northwood (Bushel) Basket

First made in opalescent glass in colors of white, blue, or vaseline, and later in custard glass and carnival glass (carnival pieces have two different shapings, many colors, and mould variations), this Northwood pattern was first made in 1905. Some pieces have the trademark while others do not and a few items were gilded or decorated. A popular pattern with most glass collectors.

Northwood Block

Really a misnamed pattern, this was made by the Jefferson Glass Company and is found in their ads of the time. It is found in the flared and ruffled vase shape shown, a whimsey that has been turned in to form a hatpin holder and flared out into dome-based bowl shapes. Made in 1905, opalescent colors are white, blue, green, and canary. Many items have cranberry frit around the top edge.

Northwood's Many Ribs

Unlike the Model Flint Glass example with this name, the base of the Northwood pattern is not columnated, and the design just rolls to an even finish above the straight base. Colors are white, blue, green, and vaseline, and the vases range from 9" to 13" in size.

Northwood's Poppy

Northwood's Poppy

Found primarily in carnival glass but also made in custard glass, this is the first example of this pattern in opalescent glass we've seen. The shape is called an oval pickle dish and does not carry the Northwood Trademark. It is possible other colors were made in the opalescent treatment, and all would be rare and desirable.

Ocean Shell

Still another of the naturalistic compotes with twig-like supports for stems, Ocean Shell uses three variations. Some go all the way to the bowl, others are short and not connected, while still others are longer but remain unattached at the top. Ocean Shell was made by Northwood Company circa 1904. Opalescent colors are white, blue, and green, and purple slag glass is also known.

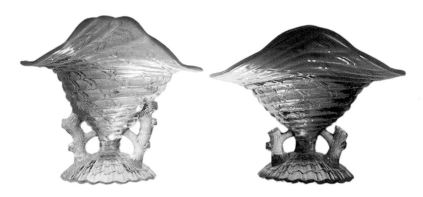

Ocean Shell

Old Man Winter

Shown in the two sizes made (the larger one is footed), this pattern came from the Jefferson Company and was advertised as their #135 (small) and #91 (large). Some are marked "Patent 1906" and "Patent March 18, 1902." I've seen the smaller baskets in white, blue, vaseline, and green, but in the larger size only in green, white, and blue. The very interesting handle treatment is a design giveaway and harkens back to Victorian baskets with decorative handles.

Old Man Winter

Opal Loops

Opal Urn Vase

Opal Open (Beaded Panels)

Opal Loops

We understand this pattern was made by one of the smaller English glass companies in the 1880s. Pieces known are a decanter, a flask, the vase, and a glass pipe. Pieces like the one shown are mistakenly called Nailsea Glass by some collectors, but they were made in Sunderland or Nailsea or Newcastle plants perhaps.

Opal Open (Beaded Panels)

Carnival glass collectors have long known this pattern as Beaded Panels. Opalescent glass collectors call it Opal Open. It is shown in a Northwood ad in 1899, so we know they made it. But it later shows up in Dugan ads after 1907, and we know the iridized items are Dugan. To add to the complication, Westmoreland made a reproduction in the 1940s and 1950s that has a solid stem rather than one pierced like the originals. Old pieces in opalescent glass were made in white, green, blue, and canary.

Opal Urn Vase

We now know this fine 7½" vase is a product of Jefferson Glass as their #18, made in 1902. It is found in white, blue, and green opalescent glass, and the distinctive feature is the flaring above the 2½" base and the ending of the striping before it reaches the base.

Open Edge Basketweave Base

Introduced into the Fenton line in 1910, this novelty item has been a part of Fenton's production throughout the years, being made in opalescent glass, carnival glass, stretch glass, milk glass, opaque, and all sorts of clear colors. Shapes are bowls of three sizes, plates, candle holders, and vase whimsies. Carnival items sometimes have interior patterns. Early opalescent production colors are white, blue, green, and canary, but later production offered cobalt or royal blue, and emerald green. These later examples date to the 1930s.

Open O's

Advertised by Northwood as early as 1903, this very unusual pattern is known mostly in short, squat vase shapes, but it was also made in novelty bowls and a handled ring bowl. Colors are white, blue, green, and canary. It is possible Dugan continued production of this pattern once Northwood moved to Wheeling, but I can't confirm this at this time. The ring bowl is known as Heart Handled Open O's.

Optic Basket

Mould blown, this basket has a ten-panel interior optic pattern, six crimped ruffles, and a twisted vaseline handle that is one piece of glass doubled. It measures 5" tall, 5½" across with a base diameter of 3". The glass is quite thin and there is a pontil mark. I suspect this is from an English glassmaker.

Open Edge Basketweave Base

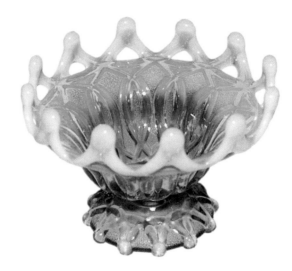

Open O's

Optic Basket

Optic Panel

Orange Tree

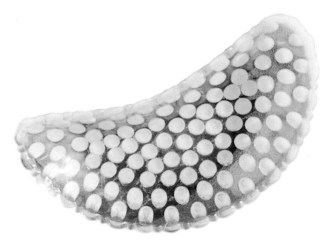

Over-All Hobnail

Optic Panel

This beautiful vase is truly a work of art with its applied cranberry edging. It is 6" tall with a 2¾" foot. It is mould blown and has eight optic panels that run from the applied base to the top. Coloring is a super vaseline, but I feel confident it was made in other colors. I believe this pattern dates to the 1890s and may well be British.

Orange Tree

I was very surprised to see this well-known Fenton pattern showing up in the mug. It is very much like the Wild Daffodil mug shown on page 148 in that it has a custard-like opaqueness with a good deal of opalescence. Needless to say, it is a real rarity, and one can only speculate if other shapes in this pattern were made in opalescent glass since both bowls and plates are found in carnival glass with opalescent edges.

Over-All Hobnail

I mistakenly called this pattern a Nickel Plate pattern, but it is A. J. Beatty's #100 pattern, later made by U.S. Glass. The pattern can be identified on most shapes by the small feet (tumblers are the exception). Colors are white, blue, and canary opalescent, and amber, blue, and clear in crystal. Shapes known in opalescent glass are water sets, table sets, berry sets (sometimes triangular), a celery vase, toothpick holder, finger bowl, mug, bone dish, nappy, and two sizes of plates.

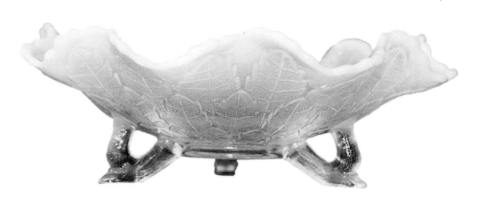

Overlapping Leaves

Overlapping Leaves (Leaf Tiers)

While it has been reported as a Northwood product, this pattern has long been known by carnival glass collectors as a Fenton pattern called Leaf Tiers. In opalescent glass the colors are white, blue, and green, but amethyst is a strong possibility. Shapes are the rose bowl (shown), a bowl, and a plate, all footed and from the same mould.

Palisades (Lined Lattice)

Here is yet another pattern first credited to the Northwood Company but now known to be a Dugan/Diamond product. Carnival glass collectors call this pattern Lined Lattice where it can be found in stretched vases and even a light shade for a table lamp called the Princess Lamp. Colors in opalescent glass are white, blue, green, and canary. Vase and novelty bowls are from the same mould.

Palisades (Lined Lattice)

Palm and Scroll

Credited to the Northwood Company in 1905, Palm and Scroll is actually a product of the Dugan Glass Company and was produced in opalescent glass beginning in 1906, in blue, green, and white. Shapes are various bowls on feet and a neat rose bowl from the same mould. The design is easily recognized; three palm leaves over the curled and ribbed feet and three very artistic feather scrolls between these designs.

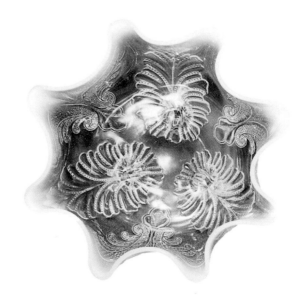

Palm and Scroll

Palm Beach

Panelled Holly

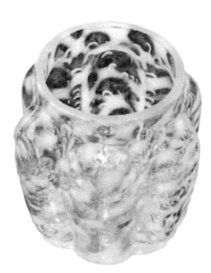

Panelled Sprig

*P*alm Beach

Made by the U.S. Glass Company, Palm Beach was originally their #15119 and can be found in a wide variety of shapes in both carnival glass and opalescent glass. In the latter, shapes known are water sets, table sets, berry sets, a jelly compote, and a large sauce dish or finger bowl. Colors are blue, white, and canary, with the latter having very strong coloring. Palm Beach dates from 1906 and was continued in production in other forms of glass treatment for several years.

*P*anelled Holly

Found in water sets, table sets, berry sets, novelty bowl shapes, and salt shakers, this pattern comes from the Northwood Glass Company and dates to 1904. Most pieces are considered rare, and the only colors in opalescent glass are white and blue. The pattern was also made in limited amounts in carnival glass and crystal that is often decorated and in green decorated glass.

*P*anelled Sprig

Made by Northwood and perhaps later by Dugan, this pattern dates to 1894 and is found in white opalescent glass only. Shapes known are a cruet, toothpick holder, and salt shakers. Colors were made however in non-opalescent glass in table sets, water sets, berry sets, and table accessories in both cranberry and rubina, but these have been widely reproduced.

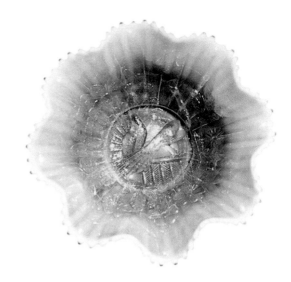

Peacocks (on the Fence)

Peacocks (on the Fence)

Perhaps one of Northwood's best known patterns especially in carnival glass, Peacocks on the Fence is found only on bowls or plates. Besides opalescent glass and carnival, a rare example of opaque or marbleized glass that was iridized is well known. The pattern dates from 1908 and in opalescent glass can be found in white, blue, and cobalt. (I suspect canary will eventually show up.) All these opalescent colors are quite scarce as small amounts must have been made.

Peacock Tail

While a casual glance may mistake this rare tumbler for the pressed Drapery, this Fenton tumbler is quite different. Note the octagon base and design that ends about ¾" below the lip. Just why the Fenton Company decided to make this one item in opalescent glass is a mystery since many shapes are known in carnival (but no tumbler!). I have seen a white opalescent example also and certainly green is a strong possibility.

Pearl Flowers

First produced by the Northwood Glass Company in 1903 or 1904, this aptly named pattern isn't appreciated as much as it might be. All shapes are from the same mould with short knobby feet that are nearly ball-shaped. Shapes include bowls, plates, nut bowls, rose bowls, and even ruffled plates. Colors include white, blue, and green opalescent, but certainly a vaseline example wouldn't surprise us.

Peacock Tail

Pearl Flowers

Pearls and Scales

Piasa Bird

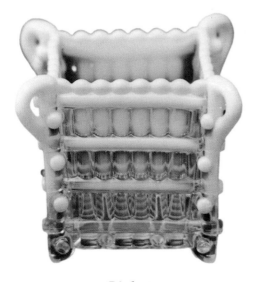

Picket

Pearls and Scales

Probably from the Northwood Glass Company in 1905 or 1906, this often seen pattern is on stemmed pieces all from the same mould. Shapes include a compote, a scarce rose bowl or even a banana bowl shape, and colors include white, green, blue, emerald green, and vaseline opalescent. Sometimes a cranberry frit edge is present.

Piasa Bird

After reviewing a copy of Cyril Manley's *Decorative Victorian Glass*, we can say this pattern was English, probably by Sowerby. Manley shows it in a ruby glass with applied decoration, but the feet and design above them can't be mistaken for anything else. In opalescent glass, it is found in both white and blue but certainly vaseline was surely made. Shapes are bowls, vases, and whimsies, all footed, from the same mould.

Picket

This very well-done square vase is English and is credited to the King Glass Company of London (1890), according to Heacock, but Sheilagh Murray declares it to be part of the Pearline ware from George Davidson. We can report it is certainly from England, found in canary, white, or blue opalescent glass. It is 4" square and stands 3½" tall.

Plain Jane

I'm relatively sure this pattern came from the Dugan Company; this assumption is based on shape, color, and similarity to other Dugan pieces, chiefly nappies that are shaped the same. Over the years I've seen several Dugan Leaf Ray nappies with exactly the same shaping. Shown is the Plain Jane nappy in blue, but white and green were made. Production was most likely in the 1906 – 1909 period.

Plain Panel

Made by Northwood in crystal, colored glass, carnival glass, and opalescent glass, and later by Dugan/Diamond in carnival glass, the opalescent production by Northwood dates to 1908. Colors are white, blue, or green, but certainly vaseline may have been made. There are six ribbed panels with plain panels between each one. The ribs run from near the base to the top, forming knobby flames. Sizes range from 9" to 14" tall.

Poinsettia

Found mainly on water sets but also known on syrups, bowls, and sugar shakers, this Northwood pattern is also known as Big Daisy. The pitcher shapes vary from a semi-cannonball type to three other tankard styles, and even a ring-necked one. Poinsettia dates from 1902 and can be found in white, cranberry, blue, green, and rarely canary. The tumblers are found in both pressed and blown examples and the bowl, which was made for use in a bride's basket, is most often found without a metal frame. Both the shaker and syrup are quite rare in any color and the tall tankard pitchers are very desirable.

Plain Jane

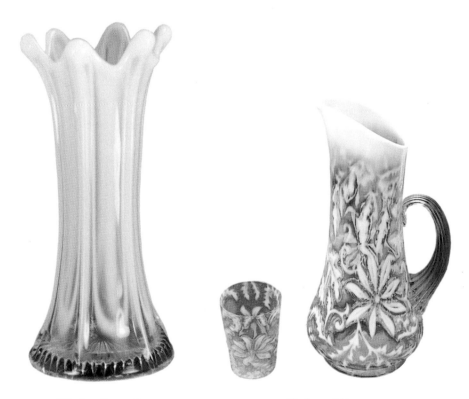

Plain Panel   *Poinsettia*

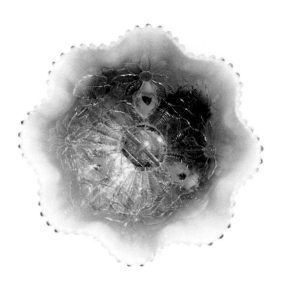

Poinsettia Lattice

Popsicle Sticks

Pressed Coinspot

Poinsettia Lattice

Made by Northwood Glass, this very beautiful bowl pattern is known in carnival circles as Lattice and Poinsettia, where it is a somewhat rare and very prized pattern. In opalescent glass the colors are limited to white, blue, and vaseline. Production at the Northwood factory dates to 1907, and the latticework is exactly like that of a sister pattern called Cherry Lattice that followed a few years later in other types of glass.

Popsicle Sticks

Credited to the Jefferson Glass Company, this is their #263 pattern. In design, it is a simple series of wide unstippled rays that fan out from the center of the bowl shape. Colors are white, blue, and green opalescent glass, and it is found on large bowl shapes with a pedestal base. Shapes may be widely varied including ruffled edges, a banana bowl shape, and even a squared shape.

Pressed Coinspot (#617)

First shown in a 1901 National Glass catalog, this compote (advertised as a card tray) was continued as a Dugan pattern, showing up in their ad for an Oriental assortment, labeled #617. In the vase shape, it later became known as Concave Columns and in carnival glass it is simply called Coinspot. Shapes from the same mould are tall vases, compotes, goblets, and a stemmed banana boat shape. Colors in opalescent glass are white, blue, green, and canary.

Princess Diana

Princess Diana

Made by Davidson of England, this pattern was from 1890 and is also known as Suite 1890 or Queen Anne. Shapes include a crimped oval plate (8", 10" and 12"), crimped round plate (7", 8½", 10½", 12"), crimped round dish (6", 7½", 9", 10½"), crimped oval dish (10½"), covered butterdish, creamer, footed sugar, biscuit jar and plate, water set (pitcher in both pint and half-pint), salad bowl, and water platter. Colors in opalescent glass are the usual blue and canary.

Prince William

Shown is the breakfast set or the open sugar and creamer, made by Davidson. Covered sugars were just not part of English glass production. This very attractive pattern can also be found in a beautiful oval plate and water set. Colors, as with most English opalescent glass production, are blue and canary.

Prince William

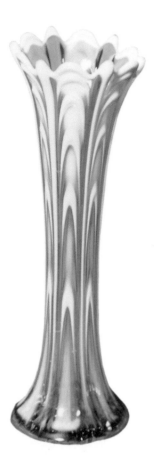

Pulled Loop

Pump and Trough

Pussy Willow

Pulled Loop

Made by Dugan/Diamond as early as 1906 in opalescent glass, this vase pattern is well known to carnival glass collectors too. Opalescent pieces are limited and found in white, green, or blue. Sizes range from 9" to 14" in height and there are at least two base sizes, 3" diameter and 5" diameter. There are six ribs with very extended tops and six rows of panels that contain the loops. The Pulled Loop pattern was advertised as #1030.

Pump and Trough

Shown in a 1900 Pitkin and Brooks catalog along with other Northwood Glass Company items, the very interesting Pump and Trough pieces are listed as #566 and #567, respectively. Colors listed are white, blue, and canary. The design of these items typifies the trend toward naturalism in so many Northwood glass products (Grapevine Clusters, Ocean Shell, Leaf Chalice, and even the Dolphin compote), a trend that continued into their carnival production to some degree with the famous Town Pump. Of course, as with many good things, the Pump and Trough has been widely reproduced, so beware of pumps with flat tops!

Pussy Willow

This little vase stands 4½" tall. The shape is somewhat like one in the Dugan/Diamond Pompeian and Japanese assortment advertised in 1906, but this one has an opalescent design of ovals on the diagonal, connected by a fine line of opalescence. Probably other colors were made and there may be another name for this piece, but this name is what the owner calls it.

Queen's Spill

Queen's Spill

From George Davidson & Company in England, this very pretty spill (vase) stands 4" tall and is 3¼" wide at the top. It was part of the Pearline glass production in 1891. Colors are probably blue or canary opalescent, but so far we've only seen the latter. If you will compare the Quilted Daisy Fairy Lamp to this piece, you will find a similar design.

Queen Victoria

Made by Davidson, the pattern on this ruffled plate is actually one we show on page 125 called Somerset. Here, the pattern was registered in 1895 as #254027 and this piece with the Queen's portrait was obviously made to honor the Golden Jubilee of her reign in 1887. The portrait seems to be a form of photo transfer. Since Somerset was made in blue opalescent also, surely this piece was offered in that color.

Queen Victoria

Question Marks

It is difficult to use only one name for this well-known Dugan pattern, for it actually is not one but three patterns. The interior is called Question Marks, the exterior pattern is known as Georgia Belle, and the stem has a Dugan pattern called Puzzle! These compotes are mostly known in carnival glass, but here is the very rare example in a beautiful blue opalescent glass. I suspect it may have been made in white opalescent also, but no examples have been verified at this time. It was reproduced in vaseline.

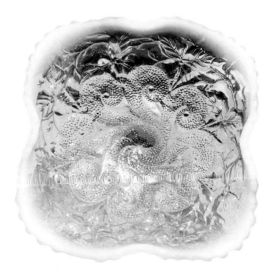

Question Marks

Quilted Daisy Fairy Lamp

Quilted Pillow Sham

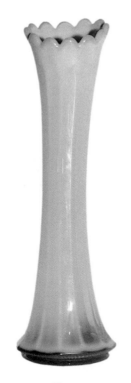

Ray

Quilted Daisy Fairy Lamp

Anyone who doesn't appreciate this beauty just doesn't like opalescent glass. It is English, I'm sure, and has a super canary color. The base is hard to see since it is a plain color without any milky finish. The design is one of diamonds bordered by sections of daisy filler with a skirt of points below a similar band of points. I believe this piece dates to the 1890s and was probably made in white and blue as well as canary.

Quilted Pillow Sham

Known as Pattern 900 by some collectors and made in 1893, this design that was named Quilted Pillow Sham by Heacock in 1983 seems to bear no Rd number. It can be found in a creamer, covered butter dish, and a two-handled open sugar, all in vaseline opalescent. No maker has been recognized, but the petticoat base leads us to believe it may have been a product of the Davidson Company.

Ray

We now know this pattern was from Co-operative Flint Glass and was advertised in crystal and gilded crystal in 1904, but this company isn't known for making opalescent glass until the 1920s. At any rate, we've seen this vase in a dark blue, a dark green, and white opalescent glass. The example shown is 13" tall and has a 3½" base diameter.

Rayed Heart

Rayed Heart

Often credited to the Dominion Glass Company of Canada, the opalescent pieces certainly came from Jefferson Glass in this country before the moulds traveled north. Dating from 1910, this pretty compote came in blue, green, and white in opalescent glass and can be found in crystal also, probably Canadian. I know of no other shapes or colors.

Rayed Jane

Exactly like the Plain Jane stemmed nappy shown on page 105, except this one has scalloped edges and interior rays. This nappy is another Dugan/Diamond piece. Just why a glass company would make two such similar pieces has always been a mystery but both are quite attractive. The Rayed Jane nappy comes in the 1909 – 1914 era and was made in white and green opalescent too.

Rayed Jane

Reflecting Diamonds

Let me say again, while they were both Dugan patterns, Reflecting Diamonds is not the same pattern as Compass. Having said that, please note Reflecting Diamonds appears in bowl shapes only and has been found as early as 1905 in Butler Brothers ads featuring Dugan/Diamond patterns. Like so many geometric patterns, this one has a series of diamonds filled with a file pattern bordered by fan shapes standing back-to-back between the diamonds. The base has the exact overlapping star design as that found on the Compass base.

Reflecting Diamonds

Regal

Reverse Drapery

Reverse Swirl

Regal

This pattern is certainly rightly named for it has a regal look. It was made by the Northwood Company in 1905, and some pieces are marked. Regal can be found in table sets, water sets, berry sets, salt shakers, and cruets in white, green, and blue opalescent glass as well as in crystal and emerald green glass with gilding. The pattern was also known as Blocked Midriff, but the Regal name is more widely used.

Reverse Drapery

This bowl in this well-known Fenton pattern was also pulled into a vase that is often confused with the similar Boggy Bayou pattern, also from Fenton. In carnival glass, the Reverse Drapery pattern is called Cut Arcs, further adding to the confusion. Opalescent colors in Reverse Drapery are white, blue, green, and amethyst. An occasional plate can be found also.

Reverse Swirl

Made by the Buckeye Glass Company of Martins Ferry, Ohio, and later in some degree by the Model Flint Glass Company of Albany, Indiana, this beautiful pattern dates from 1888. The lamp shown is from Buckeye and was made in two sizes. It is considered quite rare. Other shapes found are water sets, cruet, table sets, berry sets, salt shakers, syrups, sugar shaker, custard cup, mustard pot, toothpick holder, night lamps, a finger bowl, water bottles in two sizes, a caster set (four pieces in metal holder), and a very scarce tall salt shaker. Colors are white, blue, canary, and cranberry, and occasionally some items are satin finished.

*R*ib and Big Thumbprints

Shown in a Butler Brothers ad in 1906 for Dugan/Diamond, this vase also appears in a 1908 Jefferson ad in the same catalog! The design of four ribs in five columns with spots of opalescence between must have been a popular one for both companies, and it appears to be another example of copying what sells. Colors are green, white, and blue opalescent.

*R*ibbed (Opal) Lattice

This is probably a Northwood Glass pattern but may have been an earlier LaBelle Glass product. It is found in water sets, a cruet, salt shakers, syrup, table set, berry set, toothpick holder, sugar shakers in two sizes, and a celery vase. Colors are white, blue, and cranberry.

*R*ibbed Beaded Cable

Just like the regular Beaded Cable pieces made by the Northwood Glass Company in 1904, this one has added interior ribbing. Found on both opalescent pieces and carnival items, this ribbed version is much scarcer than the plain interior pieces and adds to the new items for collectors to add to their collections. Colors in opalescent glass are blue, green, white, and canary.

Rib and Big Thumbprints   *Ribbed (Opal) Lattice*

Ribbed Beaded Cable

Ribbed Spiral

Rib Optic   *Richelieu*

Ribbed Spiral

From Model Flint Glass (1899–1902) this was their #9ll and was found in crystal as well as white, blue, and canary opalescent glass. Shapes are many and include 4", 7", 8", 9" and 10" bowls (either round or square), a table set, celery vase, 7¾", 9¼", and 11" plates, a salt and pepper, toothpick holder, water set, custard cup, jelly compote, lemonade glass and vases that range 4" to 21" tall.

Rib Optic

The Fenton Company made this pattern in 1927 in the bedroom set or tumble-up (the tumbler is missing) in green, vaseline, blue, and the light cranberry shown. The water bottle is 6" tall and has a base diameter of 3½".

Richelieu

Made by Davidson of England with an RD number of 96945 or 96943. Shapes include a jelly compote, creamer, divided dish, biscuit jar, handled basket, handled fold basket, oval bowl, oval dish, square basket, salad bowl, handled nappy, footed sugar, tumbler, pitcher, and probably a water tray. Colors are blue, white, and canary in opalescent glass.

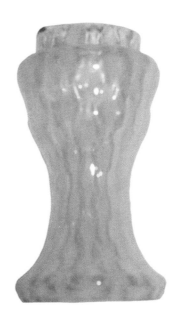

Ric-Rac

Ric-Rac

Missing its lid, this unusual blown jar in vaseline stands 8¼" tall and has a pontil mark on the base. The glass is very thin, and I suspect it is English. If anyone knows it by another name, I'd be interested in hearing from them. It may well have been made in other colors, including white and blue.

Ring Handled Basket

With the same basic design as Opal Open (Beaded Panels), this center-handled basket is nonetheless a fine item. The same design is found on salt shakers. Colors are white, blue, green, and vaseline, and the white opalescent may sometimes have a clambroth effect. The Ring Handled Basket measures 7½" wide. It was made by Dugan/Diamond, we believe, but may have also been a Northwood product.

Ring Handled Basket

Ripple

I must apologize to all the collectors I've told this vase didn't exist when their vases had to be Ribbed Spiral ones. These scarce Ripple vases, made by Imperial, have a many rayed base and are more flared at the top. Colors reported so far are blue, vaseline, and green, but surely white was also made. Of course, this was a very popular carnival glass design, made in at least four base diameters and many carnival colors.

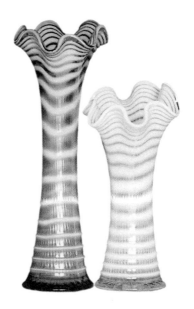

Ripple

Rococo

Rose Show

Rose Spatter

Rococo

In the last edition of this book, we showed a square ruffled bowl in this pattern. Here is the 10" plate that is also ruffled with a candy ribbon edge. Rococo is a blown pattern (mould blown) that dates to 1890 or thereabouts. In design it resembles the Arabian Nights pattern made by Northwood. We've heard of only white opalescent pieces, but certainly other colors may exist.

Rose Show

Known primarily as a carnival glass pattern, this very beautiful bowl can also be found in limited amounts in white and blue opalescent glass. Reputed to be a Northwood pattern, the bowl has a reverse pattern of Woven Wonder, a spin-off design of Frosted Leaf and Basketweave.

Rose Spatter

I am told by a reputable dealer and researcher that this very attractive pitcher with a ball shape came from either the Beaumont Glass Company or the Buckeye Company, both of Martins Ferry, Ohio. I haven't been able to verify either as the maker at this time. The coloring is much like the finish found on Northwood's Leaf Mold items called "tortoise shell spatter." At any rate, it's a super pitcher, and I believe it dates to the 1890s.

Rose Spray

Found mostly in carnival glass, this Fenton compote can also be seen on rare occasions on opalescent glass. Colors are white (French), blue, or amethyst, and all are scarce. Production dates from 1910 to 1914. The design of a stem, leaves, and a rose is little more than a line drawing and is very hard to see.

Rose Spray

Roulette

Made by the Northwood Company and shown in one of their ads in a Lyon Brothers 1906 glass catalog, this is not one of their better designs and consists of a series of ovals that are bordered by beading, with a stylized three-petal flower between each. Opalescent colors are the usual white, blue, or green. All pieces are dome-based and from the same mould, despite a variety of shapings.

Roulette

Royal Jubilee

Credited to Greener & Company, this British pattern can be found in blue, vaseline, or amber opalescent glass. The shape is a footed novelty basket (other shapes probably exist) with a scroll curling on each end of the elongated piece. The pattern somewhat resembles a zipper design.

Royal Jubilee

Royal Scandal

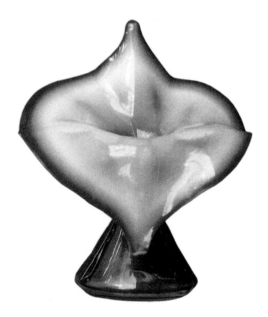

Rubina Verde

Ruffles and Rings

Royal Scandal

From England, this superb wall pocket vase is one of four designs we've seen, and all are well above the ordinary in the glassmaker's art. Royal Scandal has no RD number but most of these pieces were made in the 1880s or early 1890s by various makers. The design is a series of rope-like strips over a shell and flower pattern. Royal Scandal is known in blue, canary, and white opalescent glass, and some are found with felt-backed mounting pieces.

Rubina Verde

Made by the Hobbs, Brockunier Company in the 1880s and actually a combination of canary and ruby glass, with the ruby plated over the canary or portions thereof. Some pieces are acid finished. Shown is a 6½" tall jack-in-the-pulpit vase with opalescence on the reverse of the throat, but other patterns such as DewDrop (Hobnail) were made in this formula. All are truly fine pieces of art glass at its best.

Ruffles and Rings

Originally another of the Jefferson Glass patterns that came into the Northwood production orbit, the opalescent version appears to have been made in 1906 and after. In carnival glass, the pattern has been found as an exterior one with such designs as Rosette and even on a rare flint opalescent bowl with no interior pattern, marigold iridizing, and an added floral border edging. Colors in opalescent glass are white, blue, and green.

Ruffles and Rings with Daisy Band

Just why the Northwood Company decided to do this variant of the Ruffles and Rings pattern is a mystery, but here they've added a classy banding of daisies along the outer edge. Since both Jefferson and Northwood are credited with Ruffles and Rings, perhaps the unbanded pieces are Jefferson's that were later made by Northwood who then added the band. At any rate, Northwood later made both versions in carnival glass and a very rare example of marigold with an opalescent daisy band exists. Opalescent colors are the usual white, blue, and green.

Ruffles and Rings with Daisy Band

Salmon

According to Cyril Manley in his book *Decorative English Glass*, this fish bowl was made by Molineaux Webb Glass Works in 1885 with a registry number of 29781. It is found in white opalescent glass as well as the canary opalescent shown. Manley calls it a posy bowl. Molineaux Webb was a glass factory in Manchester, England.

Salmon

Scheherezade

While the maker of this very pretty pattern has not been confirmed, I really believe we need look no further than the Dugan/Diamond Company. Found primarily in bowls, the opalescent colors are white, blue, and green. The design of file triangles, finecut triangles, and hobstars is a close cousin to Dugan's Reflecting Diamonds but has more than enough difference to distinguish it from any other pattern. Scheherezade is a rather scarce pattern but well worth looking for.

Scheherezade

Scroll with Acanthus

Sea Scroll

Sea Spray

Scroll with Acanthus

Credited to the Northwood Company, Scroll with Acanthus can be found in water sets, table sets, berry sets, a jelly compote, salt shaker, toothpick holder, and cruet. Colors are white, blue, and canary opalescent glass with some novelties in green opalescent, crystal, and purple slag, as well as decorated green and blue crystal. Production dates from 1903.

Sea Scroll

Since the last book, we've seen this piece in a book section devoted to Davidson glass so we now know it was made by that company in England. Pieces include the compote shown as well as one on a very short stem that would be called a dessert in this country. Colors known are white, blue, green, and canary in opalescent glass and all are beautiful. The compote shape measures 4¾" tall, with a base diameter of 2⅝". The shorter piece is 3¼" tall.

Sea Spray

Made by the Jefferson Glass Company in 1906 – 1907, this was their #192 pattern. The only shape reported is the very attractive nappy, and the colors are the usual white, green, and blue opalescent. The design is somewhat similar to the S-Repeat but has an interesting beading added below the "S" and sections of line filler above.

Seaweed

*S*eaweed

First made by Hobbs, Brockunier in water sets, a salt shaker, a syrup, table sets, berry sets, a barber bottle, a sugar shaker, a pickle caster, a cruet, and two sizes of oil bottle, this pattern has become confused with a pattern called Coral Reef. The differences lie in the shaping of the small bulb and line patterns and if you will make a comparison of both, you will be able to instantly tell them apart. Hobbs made both patterns and Coral Reef was also made by Beaumont and possibly Northwood a few years after the Hobbs production. Colors in Seaweed are white, blue, and cranberry.

*S*erpent Threads Epergne

This stately epergne stands 23" tall. The glass is very thin and fine, and each lily fits into a brass holder. Both opalescence and edges of cranberry frit add to the beauty, and the lilies are decorated with glass banding. Probably European and possibly from Italy, but we have no proof.

*S*hell (Beaded Shell)

While this Dugan pattern is known as Shell in opalescent glass, collectors of carnival and other types of glass recognize it as the Beaded Shell pattern. It was made in 1905, in a host of shapes including water sets, berry sets, cruet, toothpick holder, salt shaker, mug, rare compotes, and cruet set. Colors are white, green, blue, canary, electric blue, and apple green plus carnival colors. Has been reproduced by Mosser.

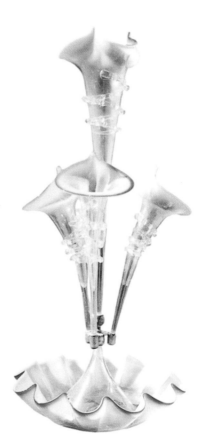

Serpent Threads Epergne

Shell (Beaded Shell)

Shell and Dots

Shell and Wild Rose

Silver Overlay Vase

Shell and Dots

Made by the Jefferson Company, Shell and Dots is nothing more than the well-known Beaded Fans pattern with a series of bubble-like dots on the base. Made in 1905, this pattern can be found in white, green, and blue opalescent.

Shell and Wild Rose

Called Wild Rose by carnival glass collectors, this is a 1906 pattern from the Northwood Company. The Wild Rose pattern is exterior, but the interior can be plain or with a stippled ray design of which there are two variations. Opalescent colors are white, blue, green, and the very rare vaseline shown. The open edged inverted heart border is a real piece of mould maker's art.

Silver Overlay Vase

Several companies made silver overlay treatments of glass, including Westmoreland, Cambridge, and Heisey, but the vase shown here was made at the Dugan/Diamond factory and has an added treat of opalescent glass. The example here is about 7" tall and is really the Dugan's Junior JIP vase shown elsewhere with a silver overlay treatment!

Simple Simon

Simple Simon

Carnival glass collectors know this pattern as Graceful. It was a product of the Northwood Company dating from 1908 – 1909. In carnival glass, it is made in most Northwood non-pastel colors, but in opalescent glass the colors are limited to green, white, and a scarce blue. While the design isn't too well planned, the compote's shape adds class, and the workmanship is quality.

Singing Birds

As I've stated in the first edition of this book, this is a famous Northwood pattern, well known in carnival glass in many shapes and also produced in custard and clear glass with decoration. In opalescent glass, the only shape known is the rare mug shape in blue, white, and vaseline advertised in 1907.

Singing Birds

Single Lily Spool

We now know this pattern is from Jefferson Glass and as I said in the first edition of this book, the metal holder has an Art Deco look. Colors now reported are green, white, and blue and the opalescence is just fantastic on all I've seen. I believe the holder was made to be used with other lily horns as well as this one, and so be alert for what may be out there.

Single Lily Spool

Single Poinsettia

Sir Lancelot

Smooth Rib

Single Poinsettia

While I haven't learned very much about this previously unreported pattern, all indications gathered from the shape of the bowl, fluting, the design itself, and the plain marie seem to point to the Dugan/Diamond concern as a possible maker. If so, I'm confident the piece was made in other colors, probably blue and green; it is also possible this piece had a goofus treatment at one time. At any rate, it is a rare item and very attractive.

Sir Lancelot

Advertised in a Butler Brothers ad in 1906 along with several well-known Northwood patterns, including Shell and Wild Rose, Diamond Point, and Hilltop Vines, Sir Lancelot is now recognized as a Northwood product. The shapes are novelty bowls with a dome base in white, blue, and green opalescent glass. The design, three fleur-de-lis and three starburst figures on a stippled background, is very interesting and quite attractive. The dome base is rayed.

Smooth Rib

Since we first showed this simple bowl pattern, we've seen it with a cranberry frit edge like the example shown, so we now suspect this was a Jefferson Glass pattern. On a collar base, the bowl has 20 interior panels. The marie measures 2½" across and the exterior is completely plain. Colors seem to be white, blue, or vaseline opalescent, but certainly green is a possibility.

Snowflake

Called "daisy or clover leaf" in trade papers, this pattern is actually from Hobbs, Brockunier, not Northwood as I stated in the last edition of this book. Date of production was 1891, and shapes and sizes include flat and footed hand lamps, a sewing lamp, a night lamp with matching shade, and five styles of stand lamps. Colors are white, blue, and cranberry opalescent. Shown are a hand lamp in white and a table lamp in cranberry.

Somerset

Made by Davidson in 1895 with an RD #254027. Shapes include a 7½" square bowl, an oval crimped plate (7" x 9"), 8" shallow compote, a 5" round bowl, a 7" compote, cake plate, handled nappy, platter, juice pitcher, juice tumblers, a creamer, and an open sugar. Colors are blue or vaseline opalescent.

Spanish Lace

Introduced by the Northwood Company to American collectors in 1899, this pattern has also been known as Opaline Brocade. Shapes made are water sets (three pitcher styles), table sets, cruet, salt shaker, wine decanter (very rare), night lamp, water bottle, perfume bottle, rose bowl, and a celery vase, as well as vases in several sizes. In addition several items are fitted with metal parts including a bride's basket and cracker jar. Colors are white, blue, and cranberry, with limited production of some shapes in green, and a few items in a canary that are likely of an English origin. A handled basket, a cruet, and a rose bowl have recently been made by Fenton in cranberry, but these are the only items that are not old. The pitcher shown is in the Ribbon Tie mould.

Snowflake

Somerset

Spanish Lace

Spatter

Spattered Coinspot

Spatter

This treatment was used by both Northwood and Dugan/Diamond on water sets, bowls, and vases, but I feel from both the shape and top design, this piece is from the latter company. It stands 9" tall, and the random opalescent swirling through the glass is quite attractive.

Spattered Coinspot

The shape of this very beautiful pitcher seems to be the same ball shape that Northwood used on the Daisy and Fern pitcher, but certainly it may well belong to another maker. I'm confident it is old, dating from the late 1800s, and as far as desirability is concerned, it would have to be quite high. The coloring is simply beautiful with spatters of cranberry mixed with the flecks of white.

Spokes and Wheels

From the Northwood Glass Company in 1906, this pattern is a well known one, found primarily in bowls or plates. Opalescent colors are white, blue, green, and a rare aqua. Please compare this design to the Spokes and Wheels Variant on the next page. This piece is a tri-cornered plate with the edges ruffled.

Spokes and Wheels

Spokes and Wheels Variant

Spokes and Wheels Variant

Just why this variant was made after the first version is a mystery, but a close comparison of the two patterns shows the variant has the area between the top of each oval notched out, omitting the blossom and stem that were there. Found mostly on the plates or ruffled plates, this variant is known in white, blue, green and the rare aqua shown.

Spool of Threads

Made by the Northwood Company, first in purple slag in 1902 and then in opalescent glass in 1905. Primarily a compote pattern, this stemmed piece can be shaped in several ways, sometimes ruffled, and sometimes not. Opalescent colors are white, blue, canary, and green. The design is a simple one but easily recognized.

Spool of Threads

Squirrel and Acorn

Here is one of the most appealing patterns in opalescent glass and in the whimsey section I show the vase. At this time, I do not know the maker of this pattern but can tell you it is quite rare, especially in blue and white. It was also made in a very scarce green. All shapes, a footed bowl, the compote, and the vase are from the same mould showing six panels with alternating designs of a frisky squirrel, acorn, and leaves. The base has a raised scale-like pattern. I'm sure the pattern dates to the 1904 – 1910 era.

Squirrel and Acorn

S-Repeat

Star Base

Stars and Bars

S-Repeat (National)

First advertised in a Butler Brothers ad of glass from the newly formed Dugan Glass Company, S-Repeat (or National as it was then called) seems to be a pattern designed while the plant was still operated by Northwood as a part of National Glass, but only released once Dugan had taken over. The ad dates to May, 1903. In opalescent glass, the colors made were white, blue, and green in limited amounts. Additional types of glass, including crystal, apple green, blue, and amethyst, were decorated and made in a wide range of shapes. In opalescent glass, shapes known are table sets, water sets, and berry sets. In addition, the goblet has now been found in blue opalescent formed into a compote shape with the Constellation pattern added to the interior (see page 33).

Star Base

Thanks to Ron Teal's excellent book about Albany Glass, we now know this pattern was Albany's #21 or "Plain Pattern." It is reported in both large and small square bowls, plate, cup and saucer, a square nappy, and a salt and pepper set, all in blue opalescent glass. The catalog cuts show round bowls too, as well as a spooner and a creamer. Also made in crystal, according to shards found at the factory site.

Stars and Bars

Glass furniture knobs were the first pieces of pressed glass made in this country and had a beginning in the 1820s, so it isn't surprising to see examples of opalescent knobs like the one shown. Today, these are scarce and finding a complete set is next to impossible. The example shown has a series of stars in prisms around the top and rows of bars on the sides. It is but one of many designs known and is found in at least two sizes. Most of these knobs are white but cranberry opalescent is also known.

Stars and Stripes

While this pattern has been reproduced by the Fenton Company for the L.G. Wright Company, particularly in tumblers, a pitcher, and a small milk pitcher with reeded handle, the design originally came from Hobbs (1890) and later from Beaumont (1899). Original shapes were water sets, a barber bottle, cruet, finger bowl, and lamp shades. Colors were white, blue, and cranberry opalescent. The Wright reproduction cruets can be found with both ruffled and tri-cornered tops, and both have reeded handles. Some of the repro items, especially the new water pitchers in blue, are very poorly done and the matching tumblers have thick, splotchy coloring.

Stork and Rushes

Found mostly in carnival glass in several shapes, this quite scarce mug and a tumbler are the only known shapes (thus far) in opalescent glass. Colors reported from Dugan Glass Company ads dating from 1909 are white and blue, but certainly green or vaseline may exist. There are two border bands on this pattern but as you can see, the opalescent pieces have the diamond file designed band at the top and bottom. The second banding, a series of dots, seems to appear only on carnival items.

Stork and Swan

This very attractive syrup seems most likely to be of English origin. It is white with heavy opalescence from top to bottom. The handle is applied and the piece measures 5½" tall with a base width of 2¾". The metal lid is marked "Patd. Nov. 16th 1869." On one side is a very attractive swan design featuring cattails and the floating swan, and on the reverse side, a stork (or crane) stands among cattails with a blooming tree on the opposite area. The rest of the piece is filled with vertical ribbing.

Stars and Stripes   *Stork and Rushes*

Stork and Swan

Strawberry

Stripe

Stripe Condiment Set

Strawberry

A Fenton pattern that is known by most carnival glass collectors, the only two shapes in opalescent glass seem to be a two-handled bon-bon and a small sauce bowl. The bon-bon has been found in white and the sauce in amethyst opalescent, but surely there are other colors out there somewhere. Production is from the 1915 – 1919 period, the same as carnival glass pieces.

Stripe

Made by many glass companies including Northwood, Nickel-Plate, Jefferson, Buckeye, Beaumont, and even of English production, Stripe (or Oval Stripe as it is also known) dates from 1886, and continued at one concern or another until 1905. Colors are white, blue, canary, cranberry, and even some rubina opalescent glass. Shapes include water sets with many shapes in pitchers, cruets, salt shakers of several shapes, syrups, finger bowls, sugar shakers, two caster sets, various oil lamps and miniature lamps, lamp shades, vases, celery vases, bowls, toothpick holder, barber bottle, wine decanter, several sizes in tumblers, and shot glasses. Reproductions are well known in the barber bottle, small 5" – 7" pitchers, and perhaps other shapes. I believe the example shown is Nickel-Plate glass.

Stripe Condiment Set

First advertised in an 1889 Butler Brothers ad, this very fine condiment set, consisting of a white opalescent base or server, a white mustard pot, a cranberry vinegar bottle (stopper is not original), and a pair of shakers, one in blue and one in white, was made by the Belmont Glass Company, not Hobbs or Northwood as previously stated. This set is very collectible and much prized by collectors.

Sunburst-on-Shield

Made by Northwood and originally called "Diadem" (a superior name as far as we are concerned), this fine pattern was made in crystal in 1905 and in opalescent glass the following year. Shapes include a table set, berry set, water set, a nappy, novelty bowls, a cruet, and two-piece breakfast set as well as a very scarce celery tray. Opalescent colors are mostly canary or blue, but white exists in some shapes.

Sunburst-on-Shield

Surf Spray

Made by the Jefferson Glass Company (their #253 pickle dish) and similar to their Sea Spray pattern, this pattern is found only in the shape shown. The pickle dish was first advertised in 1906 and can be found in white, blue, or green opalescent glass.

Swag with Brackets

Swag with Brackets is a product of the Jefferson Glass Company and dates to 1904. It can be found in white, blue, green, and canary opalescent glass, as well as crystal, amethyst, blue, and green, that are often decorated. Shapes are table sets, water sets, berry sets, toothpick holders, salt shakers, cruets, jelly compotes, and many novelties. Notice the cranberry frit edging often found on Jefferson items.

Surf Spray

Swag with Brackets

Swastika

Swirl

Swirl (Northwood Ball Shape)

Opalescent Glass, 1880 – 1930

Swastika

Shown on the Diamonds and Clubs mould, this Dugan/Diamond opalescent pattern can also be found on a ball-type pitcher mould, as well as on tumblers and a syrup. Colors are white, green, blue, and cranberry. The syrups can be found in both panelled and ball shapes. All pieces date from 1907 production and are quite scarce. It is a shame more shapes weren't developed in this pattern.

Swirl

Virtually every glass company who made opalescent glass had a Swirl design, and it is quite difficult to distinguish one maker's examples from the others except by shapes known to have been favored by some companies. It is for this reason I believe this pitcher and tumbler shown came from the Jefferson Glass Company, since it matches the shape of pitchers they made in both Swirling Maze and Lattice. Colors are blue, white, and cranberry, with green and canary strong possibilities. Notice that the handle is not reeded as on the Lattice pitcher in this shape. (The Swirling Maze also has no reeding.)

Swirl (Northwood Ball Shape)

Here's another look at one of the many Swirl patterns. This one is on Northwood's ball shape in the water set. This shape was also made by the Dugan Company and dates to 1890 (Hobb production). The Northwood version is sometimes called a variant. Colors are primarily white, blue, and cranberry, although rare examples of canary are known.

Swirling Maze

Swirling Maze

The questions about the maker(s) of this pattern still persist. We know the bowls were made by Jefferson Glass and one pitcher seems from there too, but the remaining two pitcher shapes as well as the 6" milk pitcher shown haven't been credited at this time. Colors are white, blue, green, canary, and cranberry. Jefferson Glass items date to 1905 and the other pitchers have been shown in 1903 ads.

Target

Made by the Dugan/Diamond factory, this vase pattern is best known to carnival glass collectors, but it was also made in crystal and opalescent glass where it is very scarce. Opalescent colors are white, blue, and green. Sizes range from 7" tall to 14", depending on how much the vase was swung or slung out, once it was taken from the mould.

Thin and Thick Rib

Made by Northwood and found primarily in carnival glass, this very nice vase is also known in other treatments that include custard glass, crystal, and opalescent glass. The design is one of a wide or thick rib with thinner ribs on either side. Opalescent colors are white, blue, green, and vaseline.

Target

Thin and Thick Rib

Thistle Patch

Thorn Lily Epergne

Thousand Eye

*T*histle Patch

First a Northwood pattern in 1906 and called Poppy Wreath (used as an exterior pattern with Northwood's Amaryllis on carnival glass pieces), then produced by Dugan/Diamond in their intaglio line as Intaglio Poppy. Unfortunately, Heacock didn't look for these previous titles and tacked on a third title of Thistle Patch. Opalescent colors are white, blue, or vaseline, all scarce colors in this pattern.

*T*horn Lily Epergne

Standing 21" tall with three side lilies and a tall center one, this epergne is probably from Europe or Britain. It has metal fittings, much like those found on British pieces. The design of pulled thorn-like projections along the lilies and the peachy interiors of their throats add appeal to this piece. We suspect both blue and white pieces were made as well as the vaseline opalescent one shown.

*T*housand Eye

First made in 1888 by Richards and Hartley and later by U. S. Glass once they had absorbed the factory in 1892, Thousand Eye can be found in white opalescent, crystal, and several colors in plain crystal. Shapes are numerous and include table sets, berry sets, water sets, compotes, a celery vase, a cruet, shakers, a toothpick holder, bottles of various sizes, novelty bowls, and various compotes.

Thread and Rib

Patented by Harry Northwood in 1906 (the Wide Rib in 1909 and the universal receiving tube in 1916), Harry Northwood issued this one as his #305 Flower Stand. However this epergne has been reproduced by L. G. Wright in the 1940s, so be sure of what you are buying. The originals came in blue, white, and canary opalescent glass. Wright's reproductions are found in these treatments as well as opaque ones of white, pink, and blue, all with casing on the lily openings!

Threaded Grape

Mistakenly called Dugan's Vintage by one writer, this pattern, on a stem, has many differences. First, the grapes and leaves fan out from the center of the bowl rather than circling it. Then there is the band of eight thin threads that circle near the outer edge. And finally, there is a short stem and a dome base that has a teardrop and beading pattern. This Dugan/Diamond product is a super pattern, seldom found, and very desirable. It was made in blue, white, and green opalescent and dates to 1909.

Threaded Optic

While I've named this pattern Threaded Optic, it could well be called "Inside Ribbing with Threading" as well. It may well be a spin-off pattern from the well-known Inside Ribbing pattern made by the Beaumont Glass Company of Martins Ferry, Ohio, but it has the look and coloring of a Dugan product. I've only seen the rose bowl in blue opalescent, but it was made in other colors and shapes from the same mould such as bowls, plates, and vases. The ribbing or optic is all interior and the threading or horizontal rings are on the outside. The marie is plain and slightly raised. Also called Band and Rib. Three sizes of bowls are known.

Thread and Rib

Threaded Grape

Threaded Optic

Three Fruits

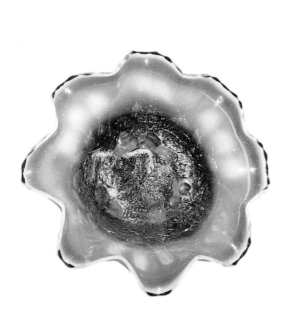

Three Fruits and Meander

Tines

*T*hree Fruits

Dating from 1907, this Northwood pattern is mostly known in carnival glass production, but it was also made in limited amounts in opalescent glass in white and blue. The exterior pattern is called Thin Rib, and the interior pattern of cherries, pears, and apples with leaves is an attractive one.

*T*hree Fruits and Meander

In carnival glass this pattern is known as Three Fruits Medallion because of the leaf medallion in the interior's center. The meander pattern is on the exterior and shows through nicely with the pattern of fruits and leaves on the inside. This is a Northwood pattern and is found on both white and blue opalescent glass and many colors of carnival.

*T*ines

Since I haven't been able to find another name for this beautiful vase (I suspect it may be British in origin), I named it Tines after the fork-like ridges that run vertically on the exterior from top to bottom. It also has a nice interior optic or ribbing. The opalescence is around the neck where the glass color is actually blue instead of the green found on the rest of the vase! This beauty stands 9½" tall and is very graceful indeed. The quality of the glass is very fine.

*T*iny Tears

Very little information seems to be available for this vase although it appears to have the same coloring as so many vase patterns from either Northwood or Dugan/Diamond. The example shown stands 14" tall, has a marie with 28 rays, and an extended ridge above the base with fine ribbing on the inside, all around the base. I'm sure this was made in the usual opalescent colors and must have come from the 1903 – 1910 era.

*T*okyo

Made by the Jefferson Glass Company, Tokyo is a very distinctive pattern that can be found in table sets, water sets, berry sets, salt shakers, cruet, jelly compote, toothpick holder, vase, and a footed plate. Colors are white, blue, and green in opalescent glass and plain crystal, decorated blue, and apple green glass. A few years ago Tokyo was reproduced in several shapes including the compote, so buy with caution.

*T*rafalgar Fountain Epergne

Smaller than some of the epergnes previously shown, this one has no large under-bowl but sits on a wide, slightly ruffled base. The lily holders are also glass, rather than metal, but we still think this is from England and have named it accordingly. Colors seen are vaseline, white, or amber opalescent, but we're confident blue was made too.

Tiny Tears

Tokyo

Trafalgar Fountain Epergne

Trailing Vine

Tree of Life

Tree of Love

Trailing Vine

Made by the Coudersport Tile & Ornamental Glass Company about 1903 in crystal (a table set, berry set, water set, and novelties), this pattern seldom surfaces in opalescent glass. Shown is a tri-cornered bowl in vaseline that has been seen in both blue and white opalescent glass. Other pieces are known in decorated milk glass, blue opaque glass, custard glass, and a rare emerald crystal. All pieces are rather rare.

Tree of Life

This very unusual vase, about 9" tall, came as a great surprise to me and made me question my sanity for a moment. I *believe* it may be from Dugan/Diamond since they are known to have made some wall pocket vases and a basket in this pattern. I'd certainly appreciate any information on this vase anyone may offer and I'm confident other colors were made.

Tree of Love

Found in white opalescent glass, this strange pattern has been recently reported to have some pieces marked "Sabino," a glass made in France in the 1920s, 1930s, and again in the 1960s. If Tree of Love is truly from Sabino, then we are confident it was made in the early period. Shapes include a compote, plate, bowl, and a reported cup. The design is interior, consisting of leaves, stems, and flowers, with the leaves shaped like hearts.

*T*ree Stump

While this very interesting mug shape is usually called just Stump, the formal name is Tree Stump. The mould work is very good as are the coloring and the opalescence. Most collectors feel this item is from the Northwood Company, and I agree it certainly has all the attributes of Harry Northwood's quality. In size it is shorter than most mugs and the very realistic tree branch handle and the knots on the bark add real interest. Colors are green, white, and blue opalescent, and all are rather scarce.

*T*ree Trunk

This well-known Northwood vase is sometimes marked and was made in several sizes in carnival glass, including a huge example with an 8" base diameter called an elephant vase. In opalescent glass, I know of only the standard size (3¼" base) that can be stretched from 7" to 14" in height. Opalescent colors are white, green, and blue and date from 1907 – 1908. Besides carnival glass and opalescent glass, Tree Trunk can be found in Northwood's Opal (milk glass), Ivory (custard glass), or a rare color called Sorbini, a blue marbled opaque glass with a marigold iridized spray coating.

*T*rellis

This stemmed tumbler stands 4½" tall. Aside from that, I can offer very little information. The opalescence forms a diamond quilting and there is an optic effect, but the difference from the Diamond pattern is evident. Origin may be England, but I can't be sure. I base this opinion on the heavy opalizing and the general shape.

Tree Stump

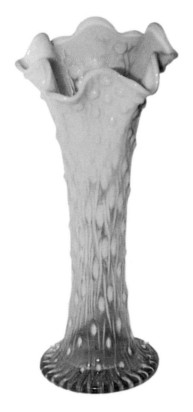

Tree Trunk

Trellis

Triangle

Twigs

Twist

*T*riangle

There may well be another name for this 4" tall match holder, but I haven't heard it. The sides measure 3" across. The pattern relies on the three-corner columns and the bands at top and bottom; the rest of the glass is plain. The entire piece stands on ball feet. Colors are primarily white or blue, but green or vaseline may well exist. Made by Sowerby of England.

*T*wigs

First advertised in 1898 as a Northwood product in opalescent glass, the Twigs pattern was another of those patterns later produced by Dugan/Diamond once Northwood left the Indiana, Pennsylvania, plant. In opalescent glass, Twigs is found in two sizes (the smaller 5" size and a slightly larger 6½" example) and is known in blue, white, green, and canary. In carnival glass, Dugan later made the same twig footed vase and a sister vase without twig feet called Beauty Bud Vase. These Dugan vases can be found in marigold, amethyst, and peach opalescent, and I recently saw a strange tortoise-shell-over-marigold example that must have been an experimental item.

*T*wist

As a part of the National Glass Company, Model Flint Glass of Albany, Indiana, produced this very collectible miniature table set consisting of the covered butter, sugar, creamer, and spooner. Colors known are white, blue, and vaseline opalescent, and crystal (plain, frosted, or decorated). A secondary name for this pattern is Ribbed Swirl. The examples shown are a spooner in white and a butter base and sugar base in vaseline.

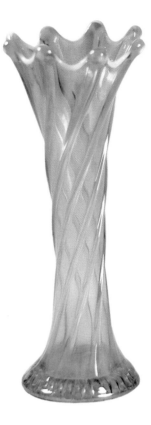

Twisted Rib

*T*wisted Rib

From the Dugan/Diamond factory in 1906, this well-known vase pattern is a spin-off of the Wide Rib pattern that has simply been worked with a twist. Made in crystal, colored glass, carnival glass, and opalescent glass where the colors are the usual white, blue, or green opalescent (green is the hardest to find). Vases measure 9" to 14" depending on the swinging of each example.

*T*wisted Rope

Our information on this very pretty 8" vase is very slim. It is a two-mould piece, with a 4" diameter across the top and a 3¼" stem. The rope decoration is about ¼" thick and there seems to be a stippling on the surface of the piece between the ropes. We suspect this vase came in other colors and would be interested in hearing from anyone who has any.

Twisted Rope

*T*wisted Trumpet

What a joy epergnes were and this is one of the most imaginative examples. The stem has been twisted while the glass was still hot and then pulled into the graceful lily shape. We suspect it is English and must have been made in blue opalescent glass as well as the canary example shown. Please note that the top of the lily goes from opal to clear vaseline again in the twisting.

Twisted Trumpet

Twister

Universal Northwood Tumbler

*Venetian Beauty Night
Lamp*

*T*wister

Shown in a 1908 Jefferson Glass Company ad in Butler Brothers, Twister is found in bowls, plates, and whimsey vases, all from the same mould. Colors are white, blue, and green opalescent. Plates are scarce in this pattern, even more so than the whimsey vase shape.

*U*niversal Northwood Tumbler

When the Northwood Company produced Alaska and Klondyke (Fluted Scrolls or Jackson), the same tumbler mould was used for both patterns. By adding an enameled design (forget-me-nots for Alaska, daisies for Fluted Scrolls), the company not only saved money but produced similar but distinctive patterns. I am showing one of these tumblers without the enameling to show the design as it came from the mould. Naturally it came in all colors of each pattern and was made in opalescent glass, custard, crystal, and emerald green. In addition to the tumbler, a similar universal salt shaker was produced for these patterns.

*V*enetian Beauty Night Lamp

Shown in an 1890 butler Brothers ad, this 3¼" miniature lamp is now felt to have been a product of the Buckeye Glass Company. Colors are white, blue, and vaseline opalescent with a rare cranberry opalescent known. The shade on the example shown is not original, but matching chimney was advertised in opalescent glass.

Venice

Shown in the 1888 *American Potter and Illuminator*, this very beautiful table lamp had a matching shade and is said to have been made with either a blue or white opalescent stripe on the fonts. They came in 8", 9", and 10" sizes.

Victoria and Albert

Made by Davidson of England as RD #303519 in 1897, this pattern is found in both blue and canary opalescent glass. Shapes include a biscuit jar, a creamer, and open sugar, a crimped plate (6½" x 9"), a water set with a matching platter, a 4" plate, and a compote. Davidson was one of three major English glass factories that produced opalescent wares. The others were Sowerby & Company, and Greener & Company.

Victorian Hamper

Listed in an 1882 Sowerby pattern book as #1187½, this very pretty little novelty basket measures 5" long and 2½" tall. It has two rope-like handles and a woven pattern that goes from the rope edging to the ground base. The coloring is very soft like so much glass from England and it has good opalescence. It was probably made in canary as well as the advertised crystal (flint), opal, turquoise, Patent Queen's Ware, and Blanc de Lait treatments. Queen's Ware is an opaque glass with yellow tint, similar to custard glass, and Blanc de Lait is milk glass. The hamper was also made in malachite or slag glass.

Venice

Victoria and Albert

Victoria and Albert

Victorian Hamper

*Victorian Stripe
with Flowers*

Vintage

Waffle

Victorian Stripe with Flowers

While this is certainly pure art glass like so many items of the 1890s, I felt one piece of decorated glass with applied floral sprays might be in order to set a bit of perspective as to where the opalescent glass craze started before it progressed into the mostly pressed items we show elsewhere. This beautiful 10" vase is likely British and is tissue-paper thin, with stems of applied clear glass and flowers that have a cranberry beading. Notice the flaring base, much like many Northwood tankard pitchers that came later.

Vintage (Jefferson/Northwood)

Found on the exterior of dome-based bowls, this was an opalescent pattern from Jefferson Glass and was later used by Northwood as a carnival glass pattern exterior. Jefferson called this their #245 pattern and opalescent colors are white, blue, or green. Occasionally the white pieces were trimmed with goofus decoration. Jefferson pieces date to before 1907 and Northwood used this pattern after that time.

Waffle

I know very little about the origin of this attractive epergne except it originally came from Germany, carried by hand aboard a commercial airline a few years ago. It stands some 20" tall on an ornate metal base and the lily fits into a metal cup. The beautiful waffle design is olive green, shading to an attractive pink just before the opalescent edging starts. The glass is very fine and thin and is mould blown.

War of Roses

War of Roses

From England and made by George Davidson & Company, this pattern has RD #212684, dates to 1893, and can be found in blue or vaseline opalescent glass. Shapes include the boat shape (7½" and 9½"), novelty bowls, 4-pointed star dish, and a 2-handled posy trough, as well as a 3-pointed star dish. Be aware, however, that the canoe shape was reproduced by L. G. Wright in all sorts of glass treatments in the 1940s.

Waterlily and Cattails (Fenton)

The Fenton version of this pattern in opalescent glass is known in several shapes including table sets, water sets, berry sets, a tri-cornered bon-bon, a square bon-bon, a rose bowl, handled relish, bowl novelties, plates, and a breakfast set consisting of an individual creamer and sugar. Colors are white, green, blue, and amethyst as well as carnival glass items.

Waterlily and Cattails (Fenton)

Waterlily and Cattails (Northwood)

In carnival glass, Northwood made this pattern in only a water set so it isn't surprising to find only the very scarce tumbler showing up in opalescent glass. The example shown is marked with the Northwood mark. Blue is the only color I've heard about and this tumbler in opalescent glass dates to 1905. I'd love to hear from anyone who has seen the matching pitcher or other opalescent colors in this Northwood version.

*Waterlily and Cattails
(Northwood)*

West Virginia Stripe

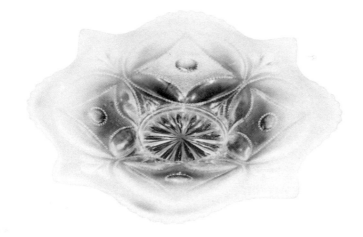

Wheel and Block

White Chapel

*Opalescent
Glass,
1880 – 1930*

West Virginia Stripe

We are listing this pattern under this title as "iffy." The shape is the same as the West Virginia Glass Company's Polka Dot and Fern pitchers so we feel confident it was from that short-lived company and was made between 1893 and 1895. This example shown has an enameled decoration and may have been available in blue, white, or cranberry opalescent glass. We'd appreciate any information about this pattern.

Wheel and Block

Shown as early as 1905 in ads with other Dugan Glass patterns, Wheel and Block has been seen in deep bowls, a vase whimsey, and a square plate, all from the same mould. Colors are blue, green, and white with the latter sometimes having a goofus treatment as on the square plate shown.

White Chapel

While this pattern from England has appeared in more than one article about English opalescent glass, I don't believe anyone ever gave it a proper name so we are taking the liberty of correcting that. Shown is a creamer, but we know that an open sugar and other shapes exist that include bowls. Colors reported are blue or vaseline opalescent. The maker isn't known by us, but we suspect Davidson. Anyone with information on this pattern is urged to contact us.

Wide Panel

Here is the second Northwood epergne design, called Wide Panel or Colonial by some collectors. It is well known in carnival glass and is equally respected in opalescent colors of green, white, or blue. Notice that the four lily receiving tubes have been moulded into the glass and the whole design sweeps in a wide paneling from lily to the base. It is less formal than the first epergne design, Thread and Rib, and has no metal in the fittings at all! The fall Butler Brothers catalog of 1909 lists this in opalescent colors at $1.25 each, and the 1913 April catalog from the same concern has the carnival glass at $1.50 a piece! How times have changed.

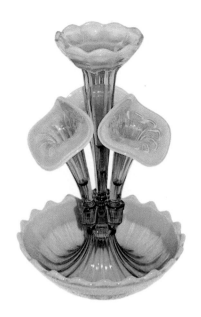

Wide Panel

Wide Stripe

We believe this shade was made by the Nickel-Plate Glass Company about 1890. Colors known are cranberry, blue, white, and green opalescent. While both Fenton and Imperial made similar versions of these shades in the late 1930s, the shaping was different. Wide Stripe is known in water sets, cruets, syrups, sugar shakers, toothpick holders, salt shakers, and lamp shades.

Wide Stripe

Wild Bouquet

Apparently Northwood first made the opalescent pieces in this pattern while a part of National, and the design was then continued by Dugan/Diamond. Shapes made are table sets, berry sets, water sets, a cruet, a toothpick holder, salt shakers, and a cruet set on a tray (the same tray as with Chrysanthemum Sprig). Colors in opalescent glass are white, blue, green, and rarely canary; other treatments are custard and possibly Dugan colored glass in blue and green.

Wild Bouquet

Wild Daffodils

Wild Grape

Wild Rose (Fenton's)

Wild Daffodils

Similar to the Wild Rose pattern by Fenton, this one has a different flower altogether. The shape of the mug and its handle are exactly like the Fenton Orange Tree mug. Colors known are amethyst, white (often with gold trim), and a strange custard-like opalescence with gilding. Production probably dates to 1909 or thereabouts.

Wild Grape

Prior to seeing this compote, we'd found only one other piece in this pattern, a marigold carnival glass bowl with a dome base. The compote is 4½" tall, has a 3¼" base, and is 4¾" across the top. We believe other colors in opalescent glass were made but haven't confirmed them, and possibly other shapes may exist.

Wild Rose (Fenton's)

Made at the same time as the Wild Daffodils mug from the Fenton Company and with the same technique, this bowl shape can be found in white, green, and deep blue opalescent glass (amethyst is certainly possible too). The bowls may be ruffled, pulled into a banana bowl shape, or flattened into a plate shape. The pattern consists of four groups of rose and leaves sections, very realistically done, with buds and thorned stems.

William and Mary

Made by Davidson of England (RD #413701) in 1903. Shapes include a creamer, open sugar, covered butter dish, cracker jar, compote, celery vase or spooner, handled nappy, oval salt, round salt, 9" cake plate, round and oval bowls in several sizes, oval and round plates, and novelty items. Colors are vaseline or blue in opalescent glass. The design is an easy one to spot, hearts separated by areas of diamond filing.

Wilted Flowers

Called "Single Flower" by carnival glass collectors, this Dugan/Diamond pattern was part of their 1909 Intaglio line. Besides bowl shapes, there are handled baskets, tri-cornered bowls, banana bowls, and whimsied nut bowl shapes. Treatments are goofus, white opalescent, and blue opalescent glass, as well as plain crystal and carnival treatments. The flower design is a weak one and looks best with the goofus treatment as shown.

Windflower

Known to be a Dugan Glass Company product that is better known in carnival glass than in opalescent, where it is considered rather rare. First advertised in 1907, the opalescent pieces are known in white and blue and in a 1914 Butler Brothers ad they can be seen along with equally rare opalescent patterns like the Mary Ann vase, the Constellation compote (pulled from the S-Repeat or National goblet shape with an added interior pattern), a Fishscales and Beads bowl, and Stork and Rushes mug and tumbler. A green opalescent Windflower bowl would be a great rarity, but I have no knowledge that one even exists.

William and Mary

Wilted Flowers

Windflower

Windflower Nappy

Windflower Nappy

Seldom found in carnival glass, this nappy by the Dugan/Diamond company is a real rarity in opalescent glass and to date I've seen only two in white. The bowl in this pattern, shown on preceding page, is part of a very small production run, so to find this nappy is a real surprise. I'd surely like to hear from anyone knowing of additional opalescent colors in this piece if they exist.

Windows (Plain)

Originally a Hobbs, Brockunier pattern, it was later produced by Beaumont Glass and dates to 1889. Shapes known are water sets, finger bowls, bitters bottles, a crimped bowl, oil lamps in several shapes, and two sizes of miniature lamps. Colors known are white, blue, and cranberry. The beautiful pitcher shown has the square top and is a sight to behold.

Windows (Swirled)

Also made by Hobbs, Brockunier, this pattern is sometimes called Hobbs Swirl. The swirl is in the moulding of the glass and can be found in white, blue, and cranberry opalescent. Shapes reported are water sets, cruets, salt shakers, a syrup, table sets, a finger bowl, berry sets, a sugar shaker, a mustard pot, a toothpick holder, and a celery vase. Strangely, the shapes in this pattern all seem to have an oval shape. Production started in 1889.

Windows (Plain)

Windows (Swirled)

Windsor Stripe

Windsor Stripe

I feel sure this stripe pattern is English, and I've added the Windsor to establish this. The vase is cranberry with a great amount of opalescence. It stands 4¾" tall, has a six-scallop top and a pontil mark. I would expect other colors and shapes exist and would be happy to hear from anyone about these.

Winter Cabbage

This Dugan pattern very closely resembles another pattern called Cabbage Leaf, also made at Dugan. Both patterns date from 1906, and the difference is the number of leaves, with Winter Cabbage having only three and Cabbage Leaves having overlapping leaves. Winter Cabbage is known in bowls that rest on three vine-like feet that bend back and join the drooping marie of the bowl. Colors are white, green, and blue in opalescent glass.

Winter Cabbage

Winterlily

Shown in Dugan ads in 1908, this very pretty vase was first made in 1906, in white, blue, and green opalescent glass. It was apparently one of those items made in small amounts for the blue is very hard to find, the green is scarce, and the white seldom found. The mould work is superior with twig feet turning into rows of vertical beading and a leaf vining around the vase. The lily shape has a glass twist at the top, much like the Cleopatra Fan vase.

Winterlily

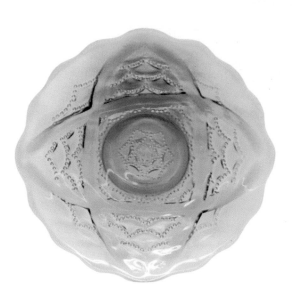

Wishbone and Drapery

Wood Vine Lamp

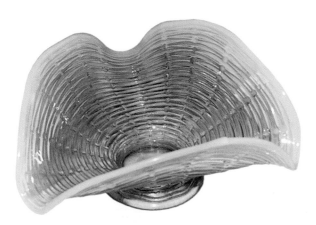

Woven Wonder

Wishbone and Drapery

A Jefferson Glass product from 1903, Wishbone and Drapery is found on bowls and plates in white, green, and blue opalescent. While the design is a pleasant one, it didn't take much imagination and could not be called exciting. However, the coloring is nice, especially on the blue pieces.

Wood Vine Lamp (With Gaiety Base)

We do not know the maker of this fine lamp but are assured it was made in the 1870s and continued into the 1890s. The font has been seen with other base designs in crystal but in opalescent glass only the white is reported (we suspect both blue and cranberry were made). For the lamp collector, this would be a real find.

Woven Wonder

Made by the Northwood Company, Woven Wonder is actually the same pattern as the exterior of the Rose Show bowl and even the same as Frosted Leaf and Basketweave without the leaf. Perhaps the latter's sugar base was flared for these exterior patterns, but I can't prove it. At any rate, Woven Wonder can be found in novelty bowls like the tri-cornered one shown, as well as rose bowls, and I suspect even a vase is in the realm of possibility. Colors reported are white and blue, but green and canary may well have been made.

Wreath and Shell

Wreath and Shell

Originally named "Manila" by Model Flint Glass (their #905) and made in 1900 in crystal (rare), colored glass, and opalescent glass (sometimes decorated). Shapes include a water set, table set, berry set, celery vase, toothpick holder, rose bowl, lady's spittoon, cracker jar, salt dip, bon-bon, and a footed tumbler. Colors in opalescent glass include white, blue, green, and vaseline.

Wreathed Grape and Cable

Named for the wreath of leaves around the collar, this was Fenton's #920, made in 1911. It can be found on opalescent or crystal glass (the leaves were removed before carnival glass production) and is rare in either treatment. We are greatly indebted to both Jack Beckwith and Kathryn McIntyre for sharing this fine item. The footed fruit bowl shown measures 5" tall and has bowl diameter of 10".

Wreathed Grape and Cable

Zipper and Loops

Apparently this 11½" vase was the only shape made in this pattern by the Jefferson Glass Company in 1908. It may have been intended as a celery holder, but if so, there should have been other table pieces. At any rate, it is found in opalescent colors of white, blue, or green. If anyone knows of additional shapes or colors in this pattern, we'd like to hear about them.

Zipper and Loops

Part II: *Whimsey Pieces*

Webster's Dictionary defines a whimsey as an odd fancy and that definition certainly fits the glass items in this section.

Generally speaking, the glassmakers were very skilled artisans and liked nothing better than to show off these skills. Often, when they grew bored or tired of the same shapes being turned out, they produced one of these odd fancies that was not a part of regular production but could nevertheless be sold as either a novelty or sometimes given to a friend or loved one as a special gift. Many whimsies were made to be slipped out of the factory by the glassmaker at the end of the day, to be taken home and presented to a wife or family member.

For these reasons, whimsies have become a very loved part of glass collecting and it is a pleasure to show a few examples here, so that the collector of today may understand just what whimsies are and how attractive they may be.

And perhaps we should also say that some whimsies were so popular they did go into limited production from pattern to following pattern. Such examples of lady's spittoons as we show here became very popular and were produced over the years on many types of glass, especially in the years of carnival glass production, until they were no longer considered whimsies!

Many whimsies, however, are a bit grotesque in their shaping and seem strange indeed to us today. Just remember, every one of these odd fancies was the product of a master craftsman in the days when glassmaking was an art. Enjoy them!

Argonaut Shell Tray

*A*rgonaut Shell (Nautilus) Tray

This whimsey item was originally the sugar base in the table set before it was stretched and turned into this very attractive whimsey card tray. As you can see, the color is vaseline but it can be found in white and blue as well. This piece is one of those whimsies that were apparently quite popular for they were made in some number.

*A*rgonaut Shell Banana Boat Whimsey

Pulled from the standard small berry bowl, this piece has been greatly stretched and then flattened out with the edges rolled in to form a banana bowl (or boat) whimsey shape. We have seen this shape a bit more than most whimsey shapes, so it must have been popular in its day. Colors are blue, white, or vaseline opalescent glass.

*A*stro Hat

This hat whimsey, made from the common bowl shape, is actually much prettier than the original shape and could have even been pulled into a vase! It just shows what a little imagination and a good bit of skill can do in adding to the design.

Argonaut Shell Banana Boat Whimsey

Astro Hat

Autumn Leaves Whimsey

Barbells Whimsey Vase

*Blooms and Blossoms
Proof Nappy*

*A*utumn Leaves Whimsey

Here is the banana bowl whimsey shape in this fine pattern, and most people think this shape is much prettier than the regular bowl shape. For years this pattern was reported in white or blue opalescent glass only, but green is now known and it wouldn't surprise us to see a vaseline example. Autumn Leaves was made by Northwood in 1905.

*B*arbells Whimsey Vase

This vase whimsey stands 5½" tall and is pulled from the regular Barbells bowl, made by Jefferson Glass in 1905. I've called the bowl undistinguished, and it certainly is when compared to this very beautiful vase shape, probably made in white, green, or canary opalescent as well as the blue shown. Our thanks to Richard Petersen for sharing this whimsey with us.

*B*looms and Blossoms Proof Nappy

Occasionally, you will find a piece of old glass that has only part of the design finished. These are called "proofs" and are very collectible. On the nappy shown here, the outline of the blossoms and the leaves are there, but the detail of the design is missing! Since only a few of these pieces were produced before the finished design was completed, these proof pieces are always scarcer than the normal pattern.

Blown Twist Celery Whimsey

Blown Twist Celery Whimsey

While this isn't a whimsey in the strict sense of the word, this is the first celery vase *ever* reported in this rare pattern and as you can see the top is edged with a cranberry decoration! Seen in white, blue, or vaseline opalescent.

Cashews Rose Bowl

Apparently the Northwood Company permitted artistic license among its workers, for many whimsey shapes came from this company. Here is the pretty Cashews pattern, normally found on bowls or plates, but pulled up and ruffled into a stunning rose bowl.

Cashews Rose Bowl

Cashews Whimsey Bowl

It is hard to imagine a bowl more whimsied than this one. The rim is pulled into three extreme peaks and the rest is rolled into a low flowing sweep that gives the piece an almost unusable shape. It does have a strange appeal however and certainly would be a conversation piece.

Cashews Whimsey Bowl

Coral Reef Rose Bowl Whimsey

Daisy and Fern

Daisy and Plume

Coral Reef Rose Bowl Whimsey

Not truly a whimsey in the conventional sense, this rare, rare item (two reported) is the first reported piece in vaseline in this pattern. It is 4¾" tall and has a diameter of 4½". It was made by either Hobbs, Brockunier or by Beaumont Glass since both companies are believed to have produced some items in this pattern.

Daisy and Fern

While the piece shown isn't a true whimsey, it is seen so seldom in any type of glass I wanted to show it here. It is the Daisy and Fern pattern in a shape known as a finger bowl. I doubt it was ever used as such and must have had a different purpose, but I have no idea what. It measures 4½" across and 3" high.

Daisy and Plume

What makes this footed bowl a whimsey is not only the depth of the bowl but also the very odd way the top is ruffled into angular shapes. I can't recall another pattern with this style crimping, either from Northwood or Dugan.

Diamond Stem Whimsey Vase

Shown is one of three whimsey shapes in this vase that was a product of Northwood and Model Flint Glass. On this one the front three edges are pulled down and the rear three are turned up, giving the vase a JIP shape as well as a square look. As we said earlier, this vase was made in 6½", 8½", and 10½" sizes in white, canary, blue, and green opalescent glass as well as the same colors in opaque glass.

Dugan's Diamond Compass Whimsey Rose Bowl

Also known as Dragon Lady (a terrible name!), this Dugan/Diamond pattern is mostly found in bowls, but here we have one pulled up and crimped into a nice rose bowl shape in a rich green. This same shape is known in white opalescent glass as well as green.

Fan Card Tray

A bit flatter than the Argonaut Shell card tray whimsey shown earlier, this piece shows that Dugan/Diamond Glass workers were just as skilled. This piece was made from the spooner in the table set. Two of the edges have been extended to elongate the piece and add interest. Oddly enough, this pattern was also whimsied into a gravy boat with handle that is often found in carnival glass.

*Diamond Stem
Whimsey Vase*

*Dugan's Diamond Compass
Whimsey Rose Bowl*

Fan Card Tray

Feathers Bowl Whimsey

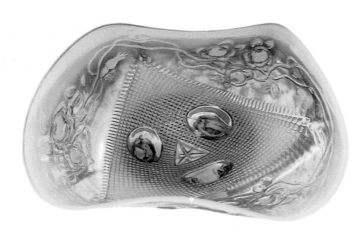

Finecut and Roses Whimsey Bowl

Flora Banana Bowl

Feathers Bowl Whimsey

Since the last edition of this book, this bowl whimsey has shown up in all colors (white, blue, and green), so it was less rare than we thought. It was made from the same mould as the well-known Northwood Feathers vase, so other whimsey shapes probably exist. The bowls may be deep or shallow, but all we've seen are ruffled.

Finecut and Roses Whimsey Bowl

Shown in a 1908 Butler Brothers ad for Jefferson Glass patterns, this whimsey is really a production item, flattened and rolled out and up on four sides. Colors are blue, white, and green opalescent glass and as stated earlier, this pattern later became part of Northwood's patterns purchased from Jefferson, then made in carnival and custard glass by that company.

Flora Banana Bowl

Flora is a Beaumont Glass pattern and the whimsey shown was made from the butter dish base. The top has been pulled to make it oval and then heavily ruffled, giving it a very pretty look. I've heard there is one of these with an applied handle spanning the center but haven't seen it. The same shape with a handle does appear in many later items, especially from the Dugan/Diamond Company in carnival glass.

*F*luted Bars and Beads Whimsey Rose Bowl

A look at this piece will reveal it is simply the compote shape that has been pulled in at the top into a rose bowl shape. As I've said earlier, this pattern has been credited to the Northwood Company, but I really believe it was a Jefferson Glass pattern. Colors known in the whimsey shape are white, blue, green, and vaseline.

*F*rosted Leaf and Basketweave Whimsey Vase

Made by Northwood in 1905 and whimsied from the spooner of the table set (the only other shapes known) this vase shape is a real find and has to be considered scarce. It is known in white, vaseline, and blue opalescent glass, and all seem to be ruffled in the same manner and just about the same height of 9" to 11".

*I*nverted Fan and Feather Card Tray

I fell in love with this cutie the first time I saw it and am not ashamed to say so. It was whimsied from the spooner and is a real find. I've seen blue and vaseline but white surely is known.

Fluted Bars and Beads Whimsey Rose Bowl

Frosted Leaf and Basketweave Whimsey Vase

Inverted Fan and Feather Card Tray

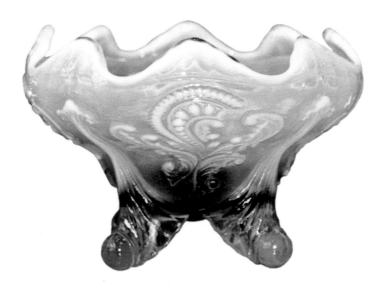

*Inverted Fan and Feather Large Whimsey
Rose Bowl*

*Inverted Fan and Feather
Rose Bowl*

*Inverted Fan and Feather
Spittoon*

Inverted Fan and Feather Large Whimsey Rose Bowl

Here is a rose bowl whimsey shaped from the large berry bowl and as such is a true delight. It was made by Dugan/Diamond and probably in the usual colors of white, blue, canary, and green which is a scarce color in this pattern. The piece shown measures 4" tall and 5½" across the top.

Inverted Fan and Feather Rose Bowl

Perhaps this shouldn't be considered a true whimsey even though it was shaped from the spooner mould. Northwood first made this piece after it had joined National, and it is shown in National ads of 1901. Northwood continued to make this piece after leaving National, too. Colors are white, blue, or vaseline opalescent, and all are collectible.

Inverted Fan and Feather Spittoon

Here is one of the very attractive spittoon whimsey pieces pulled from the spooner shape. In carnival glass, these pieces are called lady's spittoons, for rumor has it that women actually were the users! I can't verify this, but my great-grandmother did smoke a clay pipe, so maybe they were tobacco chewers, too.

*Inverted Fan and
Feather Vase*

Inverted Fan and Feather Vase

Shown in a 1908 Butler Brothers ad of Dugan/Diamond items, this very scarce vase was a carry-over at the factory and was made in limited amounts in blue, green, and white opalescent glass.

Jewel and Fan Whimsey

Known in two sizes, this Jefferson pattern has been whimsied into a banana bowl shape. Actually it is quite nice and shows the pattern well. As I said earlier, the design is simple but very effective.

Jewels and Drapery Bowl Whimsey

Like the Feathers bowl shown elsewhere, this whimsey was made from the vase mould. Both patterns are from the Northwood Company so it isn't surprising to find these pieces. Colors in opalescent glass are blue, green, or white, and needless to say, these whimsies are rather scarce.

Jewel and Fan Whimsey

Jewels and Drapery Bowl Whimsey

Keyhole Bowl

Keyhole Rose Bowl Whimsey

Lattice Medallions

Keyhole Bowl

Here is an example of a whimsey that is like the original shape. The only thing that qualifies this piece as a whimsey is the tri-cornered shape of the top and the dipping of one side of the triangle like a jack-in-the-pulpit shape. This configuration was quite popular and all companies made some bowls in similar shapes, especially in the carnival glass era. Keyhole is a Dugan/Diamond item and was made in goofus, carnival, and opalescent glass.

Keyhole Rose Bowl Whimsey

To date, three of these whimsey pieces have been reported, and all were in blue opalescent. As we said earlier, this is a Dugan/Diamond pattern made in opalescent glass in 1905. It was later used as an exterior pattern with the carnival glass production of the Raindrop pattern. Opalescent pieces sometimes have a goofus treatment.

Lattice Medallions

What a pretty whimsey this nut bowl shape is. And while Northwood was not known for items whimsied into this shape, a few examples are known, especially in carnival glass. Please note the unusual knobby feet on this pattern. They seem to go unnoticed with the usual bowl shape but show to advantage here.

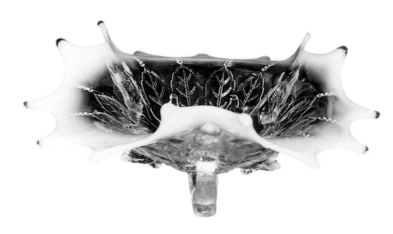

Leaf and Beads (Flame)

Leaf and Beads (Flame)

Shaped much like the other whimsey shown in this pattern, this example has the flames on the edging pulled to very exaggerated points, making this an attractive and unusual piece.

Leaf and Beads Bowl

Generally found in a rose bowl or candy bowl shape, this piece has been stretched into a rough triangle and then had the three corners reshaped to give it a very odd look. One corner has been pulled down, the other two are almost level and the back area opposite the dropped corner is raised!

Leaf Chalice Four-Cornered Whimsey Bowl

Unlike the regular chalice shape on page 85 and the rose bowl whimsey shape following, this piece is pulled in at four corners, forming a deep square bowl shape that is quite attractive. It can be found in all opalescent colors, including blue, white, green vaseline; and cobalt blue.

Leaf and Beads Bowl

*Leaf Chalice Four-Cornered
Whimsey Bowl*

Leaf Chalice Rose Bowl
Whimsey

Many Loops Rose Bowl Whimsey

Many Loops Tri-Cornered Bowl

Leaf Chalice Rose Bowl Whimsey

Here's the Northwood Leaf Chalice in one of its many whimsey shapes, and this one is my favorite. All four leaves are pulled up and tucked in to form a very pretty design. This shape shows the design to the fullest without any distortion. It has been seen in all colors.

Many Loops Rose Bowl Whimsey

While this isn't one of my favorite patterns from the Jefferson Company, I do like this rose bowl whimsey shape and could certainly find room for one in my collection. I know of these in blue and green, so I'm sure the white was made also. Of course, many collectors look for rose bowls, and this is a good one.

Many Loops Tri-Cornered Bowl

The tri-cornered effect on this Jefferson bowl is quite easy to see and typifies the crimping that gives this very nice shaping. Please remember the tri-cornered bowls generally sell for about 20 percent more than round ones, so it's a point to look for.

Ocean Shell

Ocean Shell

Not as obvious as some whimsey pieces, this Ocean Shell relies on the one edge being pulled out to form a tail-like section while the opposite side has been scooped into a small spout. It is almost as if the glassmaker wanted to form a gravy boat without the handle!

Open O's Rose Bowl Whimsey

What a pleasant surprise this pretty rose bowl was when I first saw it. I debated whether to call it a rose bowl whimsey or a spittoon whimsey, but since the top is turned in, it must be a rose bowl. It is Northwood, of course, and may well have been made in other colors like the other shapes.

Palisades Rose Bowl Whimsey

Besides the vases, bowls, and chalice-shaped whimsies, here is a popular rose bowl whimsey shape with the edges turned in equally all around the top. Palisades is called Lined Lattice by carnival glass collectors and was made by the Dugan/Diamond Company in both types of glass. Opalescent colors include white, blue, green, and vaseline, and in carnival there is a variant with squared toes rather than the pointed ones shown here.

Open O's Rose Bowl Whimsey

Palisades Rose Bowl Whimsey

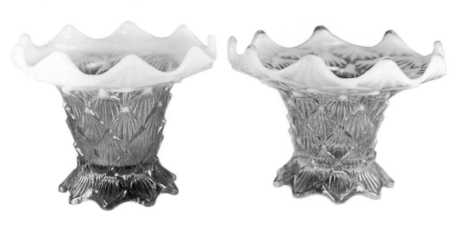

Palisades Vase Whimsey

Palm and Scroll Rose Bowl
Whimsey

Palm Beach Card Tray Whimsey

*P*alisades Vase Whimsey

Here is the Palisades (or Lined Lattice) pattern, made by Dugan/ Diamond, in a chalice shape with the edges flared and the flames standing straight upward. All colors are known in these whimsies including the super vaseline or green shown; carnival colors exist as well.

*P*alm and Scroll Rose Bowl Whimsey

Again, here is a whimsey shape that is much nicer that the original bowl shape. Dugan/Diamond is the maker, and they certainly made the right move when they made this piece. The feather-like palms seem to be made just for this shape. Colors are blue, white, and green.

*P*alm Beach Card Tray Whimsey

What a wonderful and rare item this is! Pulled from the rare jelly compote shape and flattened into a card tray on a stem, it has to be near the top of this pattern's desirability. Palm Beach was a U.S. Glass pattern (their #15119), found· in both carnival glass and opalescent glass. It was also made in clear and stained crystal and is a popular pattern with collectors.

*Pearls and Scales Rose Bowl
Whimsey*

*P*earls and Scales Rose Bowl Whimsey

From Northwood, this shape is simply the compote shape pulled into a rose bowl. It has been found with or without cranberry frit on the edge, and the glass colors are white, blue, green vaseline, or emerald green opalescent. The design is a simple one of loops filled with scales and a string of pearls above.

*P*iasa Bird Rose Bowl

The first of three whimsies shown in this pattern, this piece really shows the design as well as any I've seen. For some reason, blue seems to be the color most often found in these pieces, and I've seen more rose bowls than spittoons. Oddly, some collectors know this pattern by other names (Old Man of the Sea or Demonic), but Piasa seems to be the name most used.

Piasa Bird Rose Bowl

*P*iasa Bird Spittoon

Probably no other pattern in opalescent glass can be found in more whimsey shapes than this one. This one is the spittoon shape and while it became an in-line item, it is nevertheless a whimsey shape as are all spittoons. All Piasa Bird whimsey pieces were created from the bowl shape.

Piasa Bird Spittoon

Piasa Bird Vase

Reflecting Diamonds

Reflecting Diamonds Plate

***P**iasa Bird Vase*
   Much like the regular vase in this pattern, this whimsey has one top flame pulled into a grotesque spike and it is for this reason it has to be called a whimsey. Just what the glassmaker had in mind is hard to imagine. Surely he didn't just have a bad day, for several of these vase whimsey pieces are known.

***R**eflecting Diamonds*
   The ice cream bowl isn't an ordinary shape for this Dugan pattern, and in fact, few bowls from this company are found in this shape. For novices, ice cream bowls are round without ruffling and have a slightly turned-in edge.

***R**eflecting Diamonds Plate*
   Shaped from the bowl shape, made by Dugan/Diamond in 1905, this flattened plate shape shows the design to its best advantage. It measures 9" across and is turned up slightly on the outer edges. Reflecting Diamonds bowls are known in white, blue, and green opalescent, so we suspect the plate was made in the same colors.

Reverse Drapery Whimsey Vase

If you will look closely at the Boggy Bayou vase shown on page 22 as well as the bowl in Reverse Drapery on page 112, you will see just how this whimsey vase, shaped from the bowl, has been widely confused with the Boggy Bayou vase. The design on the marie is quite different however and starts higher above the marie. In addition, the top flaming is very different and usually has little flare.

Roulette Square Plate

Just as tri-cornered bowls are very collectible, so are squared plates and bowls. Here, the standard Roulette bowl has been first flattened to a plate and then the four opposing corners pulled to a square, making a very pleasing design.

Ruffles and Rings Nut Bowl

I apologize for mislabeling this pattern as Wreath and Shell in the first edition of this book, but I plead eyestrain from viewing so many photos at the time. This scarce nut bowl was shaped from the regular bowl shape amd may well have been made in other colors besides the blue shown and the white example I've since seen. It is a scarce whimsey and very collectible in any color.

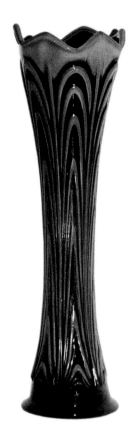

*Reverse Drapery
Whimsey Vase*

Roulette Square Plate

Ruffles and Rings Nut Bowl

Sea Spray Whimsey Nappy

Shell and Dots Nut Bowl Whimsey

Squirrel and Acorn Rose Bowl Whimsey

Sea Spray Whimsey Nappy

Made from the same mould as the round example on page 120, this tri-cornered piece has an appeal all its own. The edges have been pulled to form a triangular shape. Colors seen in this configuration are blue, white, and green, just like the round ones.

Shell and Dots Nut Bowl Whimsey

Earlier I showed this pattern in a rose bowl and that is usually how it is seen. There are variations, however, and here is one of them. Here the bowl has been pulled into a deep, square shape with only a small flare of the outer rim giving it the appearance we call a nutbowl shape. Shell and Dots can also be found in regular bowl shapes, but oddly, these are fewer than the other shapes.

Squirrel and Acorn Rose Bowl Whimsey

Just like the other shapes in this pattern that include a stemmed bowl, compote, vase, and vase whimsey, this rose bowl whimsey is from the same mould. The maker hasn't been determined at this time but production seems to be in the 1904 – 1910 era. Colors are white, blue, and green opalescent glass, and all pieces are scarce.

Squirrel and Acorn Vase

If you will compare this with the standard compote in this pattern shown on page 127, you will see just how much of a whimsey this piece has become, especially with the three flattened flames that are almost comical. But despite this odd shaping, this piece is quite attractive and would add much to any collection, especially since the pattern is very rare.

Stripe Rose Bowl

While in the strictest sense of the word this shape isn't a true whimsey, the example shown is likely British, and indeed the shape seems to be a whimsey in this production. As you can see there is no collar base, and there is a pontil break mark on the base. The coloring is quite good, and I suspect this piece can be found in white and canary, as well as, the blue shown.

Stripe Spittoon Whimsey

This beautiful piece of glass is 3" tall, 4" wide, and has a top opening of less than 1". It is blown glass and may well be of English origin although the shape seems to indicate it isn't. Many American companies made a Stripe product, and it could be from any of these, especially Northwood, but I can't be sure. Any information on this piece would be greatly appreciated.

*Squirrel and Acorn
Vase*

Stripe Rose Bowl

Stripe Spittoon Whimsey

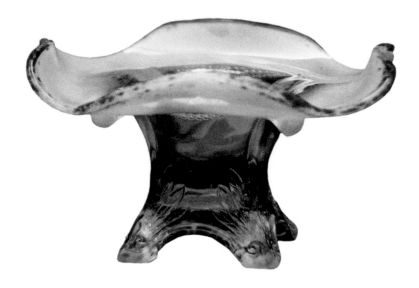

Swag with Brackets Sugar Base

Swag with Brackets Sugar Base

Just why Jefferson made these whimsey pieces from the sugar base is a mystery to me! And then to top them with the cranberry frit edging seems to be a bit much; nevertheless, I've seen these in all the opalescent colors Jefferson made and most had the cranberry decoration (a few even had gilding on the legs). I suppose they could be used as nut or mint dishes!

Swirl Spittoon Whimsey

It is difficult to say just who made this particular whimsey since just about all glassmakers had a try at this design. If I had to guess, I'd be inclined to say Northwood, but don't hold me to that. At any rate, it is a super piece of glass and worth owning.

Tokyo Vase

While this may not be a true whimsey shape, it was pulled from the footed bowl shape and is so difficult to spot once the swinging is done, we felt it should be shown here to help collectors recognize it. It was made by Jefferson in white, blue, and green opalescent glass. Some shapes in this pattern have been reproduced, but the vase isn't one of these.

Swirl Spittoon Whimsey

Tokyo Vase

Twigs JIP Whimsey

Twigs JIP Whimsey

The JIP shaping (jack-in-the-pulpit) is a popular one, and the Twigs vase really comes to life with its use. These vases with the back pulled up and the front pulled down are found in all the opalescent colors of white, blue, green, and vaseline as well as in carnival glass colors.

Twigs Vase

This Dugan vase is one of the prettiest whimsies made and for this reason was produced in some amounts although not nearly so many as to be production shaping for more than a few months. As you can see, the top has been opened and pulled into four wing-like ruffles that really give life and character to this vase and make it much more attractive than the regular shapings shown on pages 140 and 197.

Twister Vase Whimsey

Pulled from the bowl (or plate) shape, this vase is a scarce item. It was made by Jefferson Glass and is shown as a bowl in a 1908 Butler Brothers ad for the Jefferson Company. Vase colors are the same as bowl or plate colors, white, blue, and green opalescent.

Twigs Vase

*Twister Vase
Whimsey*

Waterlily and Cattail Rose Bowl Whimsey

Wreath and Shell Bowl Whimsey

Wreath and Shell Rose Bowl

Waterlily and Cattail Rose Bowl Whimsey

Here's another of the well-known patterns, this time by Fenton, turned into a pretty rose bowl whimsey. The color is a strong amethyst opalescent, one color that only Fenton seems to have made. I've seen these in both white and blue opalescent glass also, but the amethyst would be the choice color to own.

Wreath and Shell Bowl Whimsey

Flared and ruffled, this whimsey bowl measures 6½" across the top and stands a bit over 3" tall. One often hears these pieces described as novelty bowls, but to be precise, when they are made from another shape, they are truly whimsies. This piece was probably made in all opalescent colors.

Wreath and Shell Rose Bowl

Like the spittoon whimsey, this shape is made from the spooner with the lip turned in to form a rose bowl. As we said earlier, this was Model Flint's Manila (#905) pattern, dating to 1900, and made in many shapes and treatments. Colors for the rose bowl are white opalescent, blue opalescent, and vaseline or canary opalescent glass.

Wreath and Shell Spittoon

Wreath and Shell Spittoon

As we stated earlier, this pattern was made by Model Flint Glass of Albany, Indiana, in several shapes and treatments. The spittoon whimsey is a very collectible item, especially for advanced collectors who recognize its rarity. Colors are the usual white opalescent, blue opalescent, and canary opalescent as well as a very rare example with pink opalescence around the rim.

Wreath and Shell Whimsey Ivy Ball

Shaped from the flat tumbler (tumblers in this pattern can be flat based or footed), this whimsey is called an ivy ball and is one of my very favorite pieces in this pattern. It is rare and very collectible, and I wish I owned one!

*Wreath and Shell Whimsey
Ivy Ball*

Part III: *Opalescent Glass After 1930*

Wherever we've gone to photograph items for this book, we've found examples of glass made after the time frame generally accepted as old opalescent glass. Some of this newer glass is very attractive in its own right, and some is an obvious attempt to copy old patterns.

For the sake of identification, we've decided to show a sampling of these items so that the collector will be aware of them but we purposely *do not price these new items* since we catalog *only old glass*.

Actually an entire book could be filled with new items and many more are being produced every year; with the examples here we are only breaking the surface. When collecting, be alert, handle as much glass and you can, and study it (both old and new). You will soon be able to tell a difference and in most cases will not find yourself paying huge prices for new glass or reproductions.

Remember, the majority of the patterns (approximately 90 percent) *have not been reproduced!* Of course, we do not have to tell you that patterns like Hobnail, Coinspot, Swirl, and Stripe have many copies and should only be purchased as old once you are comfortable with your knowledge. Buy only from a reputable dealer who will stand behind the sale if you do suspect your purchase to be questionable.

Beyond that, all we can say is "Happy Hunting!"

Acorn and Leaf Chalice

Acorn and Leaf Chalice

Here is a brand new item we've received several inquiries about. It is a shame some flea markets and mall dealers are selling these at old glass prices! This new chalice has been seen in white, emerald green, and vaseline opalescent glass and has been distributed by a company that sells only new items, usually by a mail listing. Other repo items such as opalescent Dugan Dahlia pieces and Beaded Shell pieces are listed in their catalog, so beware!

Atomizers

In the late 1920s and early 1930s the Fenton Company made beautiful glass atomizers for the DeVilbiss Company, marketers and producers of the metal atomizer parts. Since the DeVilbiss products have become quite collectible, these beautifully made glass ones are now sought by many collectors. Shown are three examples: Hobnail (1928), Cosmos Flower (1932), and Petticoats (1933).

Hobnail Atomizer

Cosmos Flower Atomizer

Petticoats Atomizer

Cherry and Cable

Coin Dot (Fenton)

*Corn Vase
Reproduction*

Cherry and Cable

Called Paneled Cherry by some collectors, this pattern is believed to have come from the Northwood factory and is known in decorated crystal and carnival glass. It has recently been reproduced in decorated crystal, carnival glass, white opalescent glass, and the emerald green decorated opalescent glass shown. Pieces reproduced are table sets, berry sets, water sets, and miniatures of each (not made in old glass).

Coin Dot (Fenton)

Here are two Fenton items in cranberry Coin Dot Spot. The vase was their #194 and was made first in 1948, while the barber bottle, which stands 8½" tall, was made in the 1950s. Both pieces, despite being recent glass, are quality all the way as Fenton products are.

Corn Vase Reproduction

If you compare this new vase with the originals shown earlier, you can readily see the top isn't pulled like the old ones and in addition, the husks are solid glass from outer edge to the vase itself, not open like those Dugan/Diamond originally made. The repos have been seen in blue, vaseline, and a strange pale blue that had no opalescence. These repos are credited to L. G. Wright from the 1950s to the 1960s, so be sure of what you have before you buy.

Dahlia Water Set

Dahlia Water Set

First made in 1978 from the Dugan/Diamond pattern (the tumbler is from a new mould that shows many differences from the old ones) in opalescent glass, this well-known water set is one that has continued to be reproduced over the years in carnival glass, crystal, decorated pieces, and opalescent glass. This pattern was never made in old opalescent glass, so be aware all pieces in this treatment are new. In addition, table sets are also known in new production.

Daisy and Button (L. G. Wright)

One of the larger lines from L. G. Wright, first in the 1930s, then in the 1950s, 1960s, and 1990s. There are at least 70 different shapes or sizes of shapes, found in blue or vaseline opalescent glass, as well as in crystal, ruby, pink, amberina, amethyst, green, and amber. Shown is a 6" stemmed covered compote, made in the 1950s, in vaseline opalescent glass, and a #22 – 62 fan-shaped toothpick holder.

Daisy and Button

Daisy and Button

*Daisy and Fern Cruet
(Fenton)*

*Diamond Optic
Perfume Bottle*

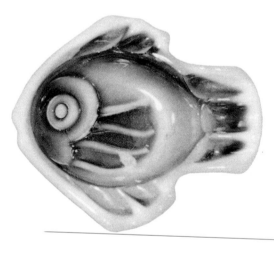

Duncan and Miller Ashtray

Duncan and Miller Vase

Daisy and Fern Cruet (Fenton)

Like the other pieces reproduced by the Fenton Company for L. G. Wright in 1983, this pretty cruet has a reeded handle. It was made in cranberry, blue, cobalt, and vaseline. Other shapes made were sugar shakers, barber bottles, and syrups, so be careful when you buy. In addition the catalogs show a sugar and creamer set as well as a tall creamer that looks like a miniature pitcher.

Diamond Optic Perfume Bottle

Here is another Fenton pattern, made in the 1980s, in white, blue, and cranberry. The globe-like stopper is commonly seen on new pieces, so be very cautious in buying perfumes. Most are new, except for a few European pieces.

Duncan and Miller

This well-known firm was organized in 1874 and over the years has made many types of glass. It is their opalescent items made in the 1920s and 1930s that most impress collectors today. For this reason I'm showing two examples of their work. First is an ashtray in vaseline opalescent glass from a line known as Sanibel. It has a very modern look, came in many colors, and certainly would not be confused with old glass. Next is a pale blue opalescent vase called "Cogs et Plume." Its artistic quality is obvious and compares with items from Lalique glass.

Easter Chick

*E*aster Chick (with Leaf & Scroll Border)

Plates like this, mostly in decorated milk glass, were very popular in the early 1900s, but the one shown here was made by Westmoreland for the Levay Company in the 1960s or 1970s. Other patterns made at the same time in blue opalescent glass were Contrary Mule and Cupid & Psyche. All are 7½" plates with decorative borders.

*E*ye Dot

Another repo from L. G. Wright, this beautiful oil lamp is a quality item and would be an asset to any collector. Just don't pay old prices for it and you'll be fine.

*F*enton Coindot Basket

First made about 1947, this basket shape has a lot of quality, as do nearly all Fenton products, but the giveaway as to age is two-fold. First is the shape, not found in old opalescent American glass and most prominent, the sectioned handled that so looks like bamboo. Remember, unless you are confident about age, always avoid reeded or sectioned handles!

Eye Dot

Fenton Coindot Basket

Fenton Daisy and Fern   *Fenton Hand Vase*

Fenton Hobnail Water Set

Fenton Daisy and Fern

This very attractive pitcher is shown in the 1983 L. G. Wright catalogs and was produced by Fenton for them. As you can see, the handle is reeded, a warning sign. Colors are cranberry, cobalt blue, and this beautiful vaseline. Now as far as buying such a nice piece, there certainly is a place for such quality in collecting as long as you know it is new and as long as you pay new prices for it.

Fenton Hand Vase

Made by the Fenton Glass Company in 1942 or 1943, this 3½" tall vase miniature was their #38, found in both blue or white opalescent glass as well as other treatments. It is still being made and recently we saw a Burmese glass example. And even though it isn't old glass, this is one of the very collectible items from Fenton.

Fenton Hobnail Water Set

While there are many, many shapes in this Fenton line made for many years (this set dates to 1952), this very nice water set is too attractive not to show. The pitcher is squat and has a reeded handle and heavy collar base as do the tumblers. This set, as well as other Fenton Hobnail pieces of the period, was made in all sorts of glass and many colors as well.

Fenton Rib

Fenton Rib

Copied from the old Beatty Rib pattern, this Fenton version, made in 1951 and shown in their ads of the time, is a square ashtray and was part of a four-piece smoking set. It can be found in both white and blue opalescent glass and the quality of the piece is very good. The boxed set was listed as their #1728 pattern.

Fenton's #37 Miniature Creamer

From the same mould as the vase shape shown elsewhere, this Fenton piece was made in 1942 also and can be found in blue, vaseline, or white opalescent glass. On this piece a handle was added to make the creamer shape.

Fenton's #37 Miniature Vase

Made by the Fenton Company in 1942 to 1944 in blue, vaseline (topaz), and white opalescent glass, this often seen miniature was fashioned as a creamer, a handled basket, as the vase shown, and also a toothpick holder. Tops can be straight or ruffled as shown, and some examples have a gilded rim.

Fenton's #37 Miniature Creamer

Fenton's #37 Miniature Vase

Fenton's Heart Opal

*Fenton's Hobnail
Candy Compote*

Fenton's Hobnail Fan Vase

Fenton's Heart Opal

Here is another perfume (minus the stopper) the Fenton Company made from 1978 to 1985 in both white and cranberry opalescent glass. Other shapes I've seen are creamers and handled baskets, but certainly many others are possible. This design is pretty enough to collect, but avoid paying old prices for glass this recent.

Fenton's Hobnail Candy Compote

While this is a very pretty item that dates to 1959, it certainly isn't old opalescent glass. Made for several years, colors are topaz (vaseline), green, blue, plum (purple), and cranberry. Numbered 3887, Fenton's Hobnail was made in many types of glass and in many shapes, including covered bowls, open bowls, compotes (several sizes), candlesticks, vases, slippers, fairy lamps, bon-bons, planters, creamers and ashtrays, wines, decanters, handled baskets, and epergnes.

Fenton's Hobnail Fan Vase

The fan vase shown was first produced in opalescent glass in 1940 and was part of a very extensive line that included a water set, table set, vases, bowls, hats, slippers, covered compotes, baskets, syrup jugs, a dresser tray, a rose bowl, shakers, goblets, a plate, and even an epergne. Colors were blue, white, green, vaseline, and cranberry. Various parts of this line continued in production for more than a decade.

Fenton's Hobnail Lamps

Fenton's Hobnail Lamps

Shown are two very different lamps with blue opalescent hobnail founts that were made by the Fenton Glass Company in the early 1930s. These founts were supplied to several lamp makers who then turned out these very attractive lamps. Colors reported are blue, white, and cranberry.

Fenton Spanish Lace

This very pretty Fenton reproduction is so very well done it compares favorably with old pieces, but aside from being marked, this piece has a reeded handle that has to be a warning! Just remember, the Fenton Company has made many patterns and pieces over the years in opalescent glass and most have been well cataloged in three Fenton books, so there is little reason to mistake these pieces. Add to that the fact that Fenton began marking all their glass in 1970, and the task becomes simple.

Fenton Spanish Lace

Fenton Swirl Bowl

Shown is a very attractive Swirl bowl made by the Fenton Glass Company in 1939. It sits atop one of their standards that were sold as both bowl stands and bases for the hurricane shades made at the time. These bases can be found in royal blue and milk glass.

Fenton Swirl Bowl

Fenton Swirl Hat

Fenton Swirl Vase

*Floral Eyelet
(Daisy Eye Dot)*

Fenton Swirl Hat

Like the Hobnail pattern, this Fenton Swirl or "Spiral Optic" design came in many shapes that included vases, baskets, bowls, candlesticks, and hats. The example shown is a monster 11" tall and 10½" across. These pieces are found in white, blue, vaseline (topaz), and cranberry opalescent glass.

Fenton Swirl Vase

The Fenton Company started making this vase in the 1930s, and it has been popular over the years. The company called this pattern Spiral. Other shapes are known, such as candlesticks, a console bowl, a 10½" triangle vase, and a large hat vase. The vase shown is 8" tall. Colors are varied, including French opalescent, blue, green, cranberry, and possibly others. Some pieces have a contrasting cased edge.

Floral Eyelet (Daisy Eye Dot)

Also made for the L. G. Wright Company by Fenton, this very nice copy is called Daisy Eye Dot in their advertising in 1982. The original pattern was the very rare Floral Eyelet, of course. Again the giveaways are the reeded handle and the shape of the pitcher (old Floral Eyelet pitchers are *not* cannonball shaped). However, there again is a new item well worth owning if you do not buy it as old and pay a new price for it.

Fostoria Heirloom

Fostoria Heirloom

Here are three shapes that were all grouped in Fostoria's Heirloom line, made between 1959 and 1970. The bowl was listed as #2183, the star-shaped plate as #2570, and the rolled novelty bowl that I called Rolled Rib as #2727. This latter piece had several shapes, including a deep bowl, and the other two items were also available in more shapes. I've seen these items in green, white, cranberry (light), and two shades of blue, the one shown and a very light airy one. The quality of all these items is outstanding and should be collected with the best of glass items of the 1960s and 1970s.

Fostoria Heirloom

Fostoria Heirloom

Grape and Vine

Hobnail Tumbler

Hobnail Puff Box

Hobnail Variant

Grape & Vine

The latest information on this pattern tells us it was not old but was made by the Fenton Glass Company in 1990. Nevertheless, it is a pretty piece of glass that may be part of the Panelled Grape pattern after all. However, the jack-in-the-pulpit shape does make it better than average.

Hobnail (Czechoslovakian)

Made in the 1950s, these two pieces, a cranberry puff box with cover and a vaseline tumbler, are very pretty examples of the world famous Hobnail pattern, this time made in Czechoslovakia. Note that the hobs go all the way over the bottom of these pieces. I've seen several items, including small dishes, a small vase, and perfume bottles, that match the puff box. Colors I know about are cranberry, vaseline, a very dark blue, and a dark green.

Hobnail Variant

I've called this Hobnail pattern a variant because of the odd seam-like sections that are on opposite sides of the piece. I've named this a "zipper mould" because it looks just like a zipper's fittings to me. It was made in the late 1940s and early 1950s in several shapes. Quality-wise, it isn't top-notch.

Keystone Colonial (Fenton)

While this handled compote looks just like the well-known Keystone Colonial made by Westmoreland decades earlier, this is a new piece made by the Fenton Company in the 1990s. It is marked with the familiar F in a circle with the #9, indicating the decade in the 1900s, a very helpful marking practice I wish all modern glass makers would use. The coloring and opalescence are very good.

Lace Edged Buttons

This Imperial pattern dates from 1937 and was still being made in 1942. I've seen more than one shape but all had the open-edged treatment. Colors are blue, green, or white, but there may well be others. While attractive, the value isn't much more than it was when these items were made.

Lace Edged Diamonds

Like its close companion Lace Edged Buttons, this is another Imperial pattern made in the late 1930s and early 1940s. As you can see, this pattern has handles. It is a very nice design, made in white, green, and blue, but again, the value is small and only slightly more than when manufactured.

Keystone Colonial (Fenton)

Lace Edged Buttons

Lace Edged Diamonds

Needlepoint

Open-Edge Basketweave

Panel Grape

*N*eedlepoint

This is a Fostoria pattern and is signed on the bottom in script. These tumblers were made in three sizes and at least three colors including green (shown), blue, and orange. They first appear in Fostoria ads in 1951 and have no other shapes listed.

*O*pen-Edge Basketweave

While Fenton made this very pattern in opalescent glass in 1911 – 1913, it wasn't made in this royal blue color until 1932, so we can be sure this is a newer piece. Old colors are blue (regular), green, and white, as well as a pastel vaseline.

*P*anel Grape

Also called Paneled Grape by collectors, dating from 1939, and found in about two dozen shapes or various sizes of shapes, this design lends itself to opalescent treatment in blue; the pattern can also be found in other treatments such as crystal, ruby glass, amethyst, and blue glass. Shown is a plate that can be found in three sizes.

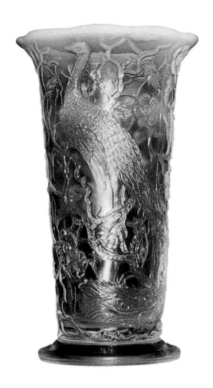

Peacock Garden Vase

Peacock Garden Vase

This very beautiful 10" vase in French opalescent glass was a product of the Fenton Company (their #791) and was made in 4", 6", 8", and 10" sizes in 1934. The moulds came from the old Northwood Company, it is believed, where a carnival version was made. Since the early 1930s, Fenton has made this vase (in the 8" size mostly) in over two dozen treatments, including a topaz opalescent example in 1988. The 10" example shown is considered quite rare and is very collectible.

Plymouth

In 1935 Fenton made a large line of this pattern, all very useful items including plates, wines, highballs, old fashioned glasses, a rare mug, and this pilsner shown. These were all done in their French opalescent glass and are quality all the way. Additional shapes were added, including a cocktail glass and a goblet.

Queen's Petticoat

Only after the first edition of this book came out did I learn this pretty little vase was made by Fostoria in 1959 as part of their Heirloom collection. It was listed as their #5056 and can be found in opalescent colors of yellow, blue, pink, green, ruby, and bittersweet (orange). I am sorry that I may have misled some collectors into thinking this was an old piece, but it is just that good!

Plymouth

Queen's Petticoat

Ring

Singing Bird Whimsey

Spiral Optic (Fenton)

Ring

Made in 1933 by the Fenton Company, the Ring pitcher is actually very scarce and highly collectible. It stands 7" tall. I'm sure Fenton made this in their usual colors of the time, so green, blue, and vaseline are possibilities.

Singing Bird Whimsey

After we showed this in the last edition of this book, several began turning up, so we have moved it to this section. We can't say all of these pieces are new items but certainly some are, and we don't want to mislead anyone to spend a large sum of money on a doubtful item. Buy with caution and only from a reputable dealer!

Spiral Optic (Fenton)

Made in 1939, this pattern was called Spiral Optic by Fenton and could be found in white, blue, and cranberry opalescent. The unusual shape has been called their Barcelona mould by one author, and that may well be just what it is, despite my finding no reference to this in the ads showing this pattern in vases, hat shapes, and other pieces from the same mould.

Spiral Optic Hat

While Fenton first made their Spiral Optic pattern in 1939, this hat shape shown came along a bit later. The blue opalescent one shown was made in 1952 and again in the 1970s. These hat shapes, as well as vases and baskets from the same mould, were made in several sizes and colors including blue, green, cranberry, and French (white) opalescent. The example shown is 3" tall and measures 3¼" across the top.

Spiral Optic Hat

Stamm House Dewdrop (#1886/642)

Made by the Imperial Glass Company in 1966 in large (10") and small (5") bowls in a beautiful canary opalescent glass, this is a fine piece of new glass work. It has the look of old English opalescent glass and since Imperial made very little opalescent glass at any time, this is a collectible item indeed and one of the collectibles of the future.

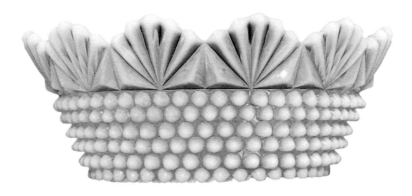

Stamm House Dewdrop

Strippled Scroll and Prism

After three years of searching for the maker and age of this pattern, we are at a loss, so we have included it here in the late glass to be on the safe side. It is a 7½" tall stemmed goblet with excellent opalescence as well as color and reminds one of the work done by the Fostoria Company with their Heirloom line. Anyone who can shed some light on this pattern is urged to contact us.

Strippled Scroll and Prism

Swan Bowl

Thread and Rib
Whimsey Epergne

Tokyo

Swan Bowl

Apparently this bowl and its companion pieces (smaller bowls and candlesticks) were first made at the Dugan/Diamond plant in 1926 – 1927 and later at the Fenton Art Glass factory in 1934 – 1939. The Dugan/Diamond version is known in pink, green, and black glass, and the Fenton pieces are advertised in opalescent colors so it appears the master bowl shown is a Fenton item despite its color matching so many of Dugan's blue opalescent items. At any rate, these blue pieces are considered rare as are the green opalescent items. Other treatments at the Fenton factory are satinized crystal (1939), amber (1938), amethyst (same year), and the large bowl is currently being made in a pretty misty green.

Thread and Rib Whimsey Epergne

Like many collectors, I was sold on this piece but in reality it is not old. It was made in the 1940s by L. G. Wright from moulds made by the Island Mould and Machine Company (copies of the original Northwood design). Wright made these in blue and vaseline opalescent glass with cased lily edges, as well as in opaque colors, and in crystal. They were sold through Koscherak Brothers. We apologize for our error in thinking this was an old piece.

Tokyo

If you look closely at the compote shown, you can see the color is light, the opalescence thin. The original pattern was made by Jefferson Glass in 1905, but this piece when held and examined is obviously not of that quality. I do not know of other shapes having been reproduced but it is possible.

Trout

When I first showed this pretty bowl, I had no information about it but speculated it might be French. It is, in fact, Verlys, made by the Holophane Company of France in 1931, so we've moved it from the old glass section. Fenton bought the mould in 1966 and has reproduced this piece. New treatments include an acid finish with opalescence. The bowl has an 8½" diameter and stands 3½" tall.

Twigs (Reproduction)

On close examination, you will see some differences from the regular Twigs vase. First, the lip has a cased edge, a clear applied edging. On some, not all however, the area between the legs and the body of the vase is filled solid with glass. Beware of these and always know the dealer before you buy this pattern. Colors of the reproductions are vaseline, blue, and white opalescent (so far); the white opal ones are also being iridized to create copies in peach opal. The old vase was never made in this treatment.

Vulcan

We can now say that all the opalescent pieces in this pattern are not old but were made by the Fenton Glass Company in the last two decades. Apparently Ohio Flint Glass made only crystal in this pattern, and the Fenton Company turned out the opalescent items in blue, green, white, and a color called peaches and cream, in many shapes, from 1980 to the present.

Trout

Twigs (Reproduction)

Vulcan

Wildflower   *Wreathed Cherry*

*Wright's Thread and
Rib Epergne*

Wildflower

First sold by L. G. Wright in the 1940s and in an expanded line in the 1959 – 1960 era, this reproduction of the old U.S. Glass pattern can be found in several treatments, including crystal, amber, blue, and green, as well as vaseline and blue opalescent glass. Reproduced shapes include covered compotes, a table set, goblets, square plates, salt dips (two styles), footed sauce, covered candy jar, and a 7½" footed vase. No old opalescent pieces exist!

Wreathed Cherry

Apparently all the opalescent items in this Dugan/Diamond pattern are new, made for and distributed by the L. G. Wright Company starting in 1963 and continuing for several years. Colors are blue and vaseline in opalescent glass, as well as some non-opalescent runs that include amber, red, emerald green, and blue.

Wright's Thread and Rib Epergne

In 1940 L. G. Wright reproduced the Northwood #305 (Thread and Rib) epergne from moulds from Island Mould and Machine Company. Fenton was the maker of the epergnes in several crest or cased edge treatments as well as plain blue or vaseline opalescent ones. These epergnes continued in production into the 1950s and were sold through a New York import dealer, Kosherak Brothers. Beware of *all* cased examples or ones with the flames pulled. They are all reproductions.

Price Guide

As in our past price guides, we've attempted to include in a complete and up-to-date manner American and English opalescent glass production 1890 to 1930, a natural time frame for such glass, one that separates antique production from contemporary. Prices followed by an asterisk (*) are speculative. The same mark (*) after a pattern name indicates this pattern has been reproduced in some shape(s). In a few instances, prices have been averaged where several variations of a shape exist, but we've tried to list prices as completely as possible.

Values in this guide were determined from dealers' lists, shop taggings, antique guide listings, and personal observation. Auction prices played only minor roles due to their often inflated bidding value. All items are priced as in mint condition and with average opalescence; flaws or poor coloring reduces value. Please remember this is only a guide and prices herein are not set in stone. As with all our price guides, this one is meant to advise the buyer rather than set prices.

Most pattern names conform to those most frequently encountered but where more than one name is commonly in use, we've included both names in the interest of clarity.

Of course, we welcome all constructive comments from readers and ask anyone with more information to contact us. Please include a self-addressed, stamped envelope with your correspondence. We are always looking for information or photos of patterns we haven't covered in this edition. That's how we learn and how we improve these books with each new edition.

	Blue	Green	White	Vaseline/ Canary	Cranberry	Other
Abalone						
Bowl	35.00	30.00	25.00	40.00		
Acorn Burrs (& Bark)						
Bowl, Master	150.00		110.00			
Bowl, Sauce	55.00		45.00			
Adonis Pineapple						
Claret Bottle	400.00					425.00 Amber
Ala-Bock						
Rose Bowl	140.00			135.00		
Pitcher	250.00			250.00		
Tumbler	30.00			30.00		
Alaska						
Banana Boat	275.00		255.00	275.00		270.00 Emerald
Bowl, Master	175.00		140.00	175.00		165.00 Emerald
Bowl, Sauce	65.00		30.00	60.00		60.00 Emerald
Bride's Basket	300.00		150.00	400.00		
Butter	400.00		300.00	425.00		300.00 Emerald
Celery Tray	200.00		140.00	225.00		175.00 Emerald
Creamer	90.00		70.00	85.00		80.00 Emerald
Cruet	325.00		280.00	300.00		325.00 Emerald
Pitcher	425.00		375.00	400.00		475.00 Emerald
Tumbler	80.00		60.00	80.00		90.00 Emerald
Shakers, Pr.	175.00		90.00	165.00		125.00 Emerald
Spooner	100.00		70.00	90.00		90.00 Emerald
Sugar w/lid	180.00		150.00	175.00		175.00 Emerald
Alhambra						
Rose Bowl	150.00		120.00	160.00	275.00	
Syrup	375.00		300.00	400.00	590.00	
Tumbler	75.00		55.00	70.00	120.00	
Alva						
Oil Lamp	250.00*		220.00*			
Arabian Nights						
Pitcher	400.00		300.00	400.00	1,200.00	
Tumbler	65.00		50.00	75.00	125.00	
Syrup	225.00		200.00	275.00		
Argonaut Shell *(Nautilus)						
Bowl, Master	150.00		125.00			
Bowl, Sauce	65.00		50.00			
Butter	325.00		275.00			
Creamer	200.00		150.00			
Cruet	500.00		350.00			
Jelly Compote	125.00		75.00	90.00		
Novelty Bowls	65.00		50.00	100.00		
Pitcher	500.00		375.00			
Tumbler	125.00		100.00	100.00		
Shakers, Pr.	110.00		85.00	100.00		
Spooner	200.00		150.00			
Sugar	265.00		225.00			
(Add 15% for Script signed pcs.)						
Arched Panels						
Bowl, Master				100.00		

	Blue	Green	White	Vaseline/ Canary	Cranberry	Other
Bowl, Sauce				30.00		
Argus (Thumbprint)						
Compote	90.00	95.00	50.00	80.00		
Ascot						
Biscuit Jar	175.00			160.00		
Bowl	55.00			75.00		
Creamer	85.00			90.00		
Open Sugar	85.00			85.00		
Astro						
Bowl	55.00	50.00	40.00	50.00		
Hat Whimsey	75.00	70.00	65.00	75.00		
Aurora Borealis						
Novelty Vase	70.00	85.00	55.00			
Autumn Leaves						
Banana Bowl	50.00	70.00	40.00			
Bowl	75.00	95.00	50.00			
Baby Coinspot*						
Syrup			140.00			
Vase		100.00		90.00		
Ball Foot Hobnail						
Bowl			75.00			
Band & Rib (Threaded Optic)						
Bowl, 7" – 9"	60.00		45.00			
Rose Bowl	40.00		30.00			
Banded Neck Scale Optic						
Vase			55.00			
Barbells						
Bowl	40.00	50.00	30.00	45.00		
Basketweave* (Open Edge)						
Bowl	40.00	35.00	25.00	40.00		
Console Set, 3 Pcs.	250.00	275.00	200.00	250.00		
Nappy	50.00	40.00	35.00	40.00		
Plate	60.00	80.00	45.00	100.00		
Beaded Base JIP						
Vase	75.00		45.00			
Beaded Block						
Creamer			65.00	95.00		
Rose Bowl, Sm.	100.00	100.00				
Sugar, Open			75.00	100.00		
Beaded Cable						
Bowl, Ftd.	50.00	45.00	35.00	45.00		
Rose Bowl, Ftd.	65.00	60.00	45.00	60.00		
*Add 10% for Interior pattern						
Beaded Drapes						
Banana Bowl, Ftd.	50.00	50.00	45.00	40.00		
Bowl, Ftd.	45.00	40.00	30.00	50.00		
Rose Bowl, Ftd.	55.00	55.00	40.00			
*Add 10% for Frit						
Beaded Fan						
Bowl, Ftd.	40.00	45.00	35.00			
Rose Bowl, Ftd.	50.00	50.00	40.00			
Beaded Fleur de Lis						
Bowl, Novelty	55.00	55.00	45.00			

	Blue	Green	White	Vaseline/Canary	Cranberry	Other
Bowl, Whimsey	90.00	95.00	75.00			
Compote	50.00	50.00	45.00			
Rose Bowl	60.00	60.00	50.00			
Beaded Moon & Stars						
Banana Bowl, Stemmed	85.00	90.00	65.00			
Bowl	70.00	90.00	50.00			
Compote	80.00	95.00	60.00			
Beaded Ovals & Holly						
Spooner	95.00		70.00	90.00		
Beaded Ovals in Sand						
Bowl, Master	75.00	70.00				
Bowl, Sauce	35.00	30.00				
Butter	300.00	250.00				
Creamer	90.00	80.00				
Cruet	250.00	225.00				
Nappy	55.00	45.00				
Pitcher	425.00	375.00				
Tumbler	100.00	85.00				
Shakers, Pr.	100.00	85.00				
Spooner	100.00	85.00				
Sugar	250.00	225.00				
Toothpick Holder	200.00	175.00				
Beaded Star Medallion						
Shade	70.00	55.00	40.00			
Beaded Stars & Swag						
Adv. Bowl	425.00	450.00	325.00			
Adv. Plate	525.00	550.00	450.00			
Bowl	45.00	55.00	35.00			
Plate	100.00		60.00			
Rose Bowl	60.00	60.00	40.00			
Beads & Bark						
Vase, Ftd.	80.00	70.00	55.00			
Beads & Curleycues						
Novelty Bowls, Ftd.	50.00	50.00	40.00			
(Beatty) Honeycomb*						
Bowl, Master	50.00		40.00			
Bowl, Sauce	25.00		20.00			
Butter	225.00		175.00			
Celery Vase	80.00		70.00			
Creamer	90.00		50.00			
Cruet	200.00		175.00			
Individual						
Cream/Sugar Set	150.00		125.00			
Mug	55.00		40.00			
Mustard Pot	100.00		75.00			
Pitcher	200.00		150.00			
Tumbler	50.00		35.00			
Shakers, Pr.	80.00		60.00			
Spooner	90.00		50.00			
Sugar	125.00		100.00			
Toothpick Holder	250.00		200.00			
Beatty Rib						
Bowl, Master	55.00		35.00			

	Blue	Green	White	Vaseline/ Canary	Cranberry	Other
Bowl, Novelty	75.00		65.00			
Bowl, Sauce	30.00		20.00			
Butter	200.00		125.00			
Celery Vase	75.00		65.00			
Cracker Jar	125.00		100.00			
Creamer	60.00		40.00			
Finger Bowl	30.00		20.00			
Match Holder	50.00		35.00			
Mug	55.00		40.00			
Mustard Jar	150.00		125.00			
Nappy, Various	40.00		25.00			
Pitcher	200.00		150.00			
Tumbler	50.00		30.00			
Shakers, Pr.	75.00		60.00			
Salt Dip	60.00		45.00			
Spooner	60.00		40.00			
Sugar	145.00		100.00			
Sugar Shaker	125.00		100.00			
Toothpick	65.00		55.00			
Beatty Swirl						
Bowl, Master	55.00		40.00			
Bowl, Sauce	30.00		20.00			
Butter	175.00		150.00			
Celery Vase	75.00		60.00			
Creamer	75.00		60.00			
Mug	65.00		35.00	85.00		
Pitcher	185.00		125.00	225.00		
Tumbler	40.00		30.00	50.00		
Spooner	75.00		60.00			
Sugar	125.00		100.00			
Syrup	250.00		200.00	275.00		
Water Tray	100.00		65.00	110.00		
Beaumont Stripe						
Pitcher	325.00		285.00	350.00		
Tumbler	65.00		50.00	70.00		
Berry Patch						
Novelty Bowl	50.00	45.00	30.00			
Plate	75.00	75.00	50.00			
Blackberry						
Bon-Bon			50.00			75.00 Amethyst
Bowl			30.00			65.00 Amethyst
Nappy	40.00	45.00	30.00			55.00 Amethyst
Plate, 6"			30.00			85.00 Amethyst
Blackberry Spray						
Hat			35.00			100.00 Amethyst
Blocked Thumbprint & Beads (Fishscale & Beads)						
Bowl	50.00	55.00	40.00			
Nappy	40.00	40.00	30.00			
Blooms & Blossoms						
Nappy, Hndl.	50.00	50.00	40.00			
Proof Whimsey, Scarce	100.00	65.00				
Blossom & Palms						
Bowl	50.00	45.00	35.00			

	Blue	Green	White	Vaseline/ Canary	Cranberry	Other
Blossom & Web						
Bowl, Rare	200.00	175.00	150.00			
Blown Diamonds						
Pitcher, Scarce				300.00		
Blown Drape						
Pitcher	550.00	500.00	350.00		900.00	
Tumbler	175.00	150.00	165.00		300.00	
Sugar Shaker	500.00	450.00	300.00			
Blown Twist						
Celery Vase	400.00		350.00	450.00		
Pitcher	550.00	500.00	350.00	525.00	900.00	
Tumbler	200.00	175.00	150.00	175.00	325.00	
Sugar Shaker	200.00	185.00	175.00	200.00	600.00	
Syrup	250.00		200.00		400.00	
Boggy Bayou						
Vase	40.00	35.00	25.00			75.00 Amethyst
Brideshead						
Basket, Hndl.	90.00					
Butter	100.00					
Celery Vase	60.00					
Creamer	65.00					
Novelty Bowl	55.00					
Oval Tray	125.00		100.00	120.00		
Pitcher, 2 Sizes	145.00 – 165.00					
Tumbler	100.00					
Sugar	75.00					
Broken Pillar						
Card Tray						
(from compote shape)	170.00		135.00	165.00		
Compote	160.00		125.00	155.00		
(Bubble) Lattice						
Bowl, Master	70.00	50.00	45.00	65.00	80.00	
Bowl, Sauce	30.00	25.00	20.00	30.00	35.00	
Bride's Basket	125.00	100.00	75.00	130.00	225.00	
Butter	225.00	200.00	150.00	200.00	725.00	
Celery Vase					125.00	
Creamer	60.00	50.00	50.00	55.00	150.00	
Cruet, Avg. Pricing	175.00	160.00	135.00	170.00	400.00	
Finger Bowl	45.00	40.00	25.00	45.00	125.00	
Pitcher, Various	300.00	275.00	225.00	275.00	750.00	
Tumbler, Various	50.00	50.00	40.00	45.00	125.00	
Shakers, Various	150.00	125.00	100.00	175.00	150.00 – 300.00	
Spooner	60.00	50.00	50.00	55.00	200.00	
Sugar	125.00	100.00	75.00	100.00	425.00	
Sugar Shaker	235.00	225.00	185.00	225.00	300.00	
Syrup, Various	225.00	200.00	175.00	200.00	750.00	
Toothpick Holder	300.00	275.00	200.00	350.00	300.00 – 550.00	
Bulbous Base Coinspot						
Sugar Shaker	125.00		90.00		175.00	
Bull's-Eye						
Bowl	50.00				65.00	
Shade	60.00		40.00			
Water Bottle			175.00		265.00	

	Blue	Green	White	Vaseline/ Canary	Cranberry	Other
Bushel Basket						
One Shape, Scarce	150.00	350.00	125.00	400.00		
Butterfly & Lily						
Epergne	150.00	150.00	110.00	150.00		
Button Panels						
Bowl	45.00		35.00	50.00		
Rose Bowl	45.00		40.00	55.00		
Buttons & Braids						
Bowl	50.00	55.00	30.00		85.00	
Pitcher	200.00	175.00	135.00	300.00	400.00	
Tumbler	50.00	45.00	30.00	85.00	100.00	
Cabbage Leaf						
Novelty Bowl, Ftd.	80.00	65.00	50.00			
Calyx						
Vase, Scarce	65.00		50.00	60.00		
Carousel						
Bowl	55.00	50.00	35.00			
Cane & Diamond Swirl						
Stemmed Tray	75.00			70.00		
Casbah						
Compote			150.00			
Cashews						
Bowl	50.00	45.00	30.00			
Rose Bowl, Rare	100.00	95.00	75.00			
Whimsey Bowl	55.00	50.00	35.00			
Cherry						
Master Bowl	70.00					
Sm. Bowl	25.00					
Covered Butter	225.00					
Creamer	110.00					
Sugar	125.00					
Spooner	115.00					
Goblet	75.00					
Wine	80.00					
Plate, Rare	160.00					
Open Compote	90.00					
Covered Compote	125.00					
Novelty Bowls	60.00					
Cherry Panels						
Novelty Bowl	75.00		60.00	70.00		
Chippendale						
Basket	60.00			65.00		
Compote	65.00			80.00		
Pitcher	130.00			145.00		
Tumbler	40.00			35.00		
Christmas Pearls						
Cruet	300.00	280.00	350.00			
Shakers, Pr.	165.00	140.00	175.00			
Christmas Snowflake*						
Pitcher, Either	675.00		525.00		950.00	
Tumbler, Average	110.00		100.00		125.00	
Christmas Trees						
Smoke Shade, Rare						500.00 Rubina Verde

	Blue	Green	White	Vaseline/ Canary	Cranberry	Other
Chrysanthemum						
Bowl, Ftd., 11"	250.00		175.00			325.00
Chrysanthemum Base Swirl						
Bowl, Master	55.00		45.00		120.00	
Bowl, Sauce	35.00		25.00		50.00	
Butter	325.00		300.00		500.00	
Celery Vase	140.00		115.00		225.00	
Creamer	100.00		75.00		400.00	
Cruet	225.00		200.00		500.00	
Finger Bowl	45.00		30.00		140.00	
Mustard Pot	150.00		120.00		240.00	
Pitcher	400.00		350.00		900.00	
Tumbler	100.00		75.00		125.00	
Shakers, Pr.	125.00		100.00		300.00	
Spooner	100.00		75.00		215.00	
Straw Holder w/lid	500.00		400.00		1,200.00	
Sugar	200.00		175.00		350.00	
Sugar Shaker	200.00		175.00		275.00	
Syrup	200.00		175.00		500.00	
Toothpick Holder	100.00		75.00		300.00	
Chrysanthemum Swirl Vt.						
Pitcher, Rare	400.00		275.00		925.00	400.00 Teal
Tumbler, Rare	100.00		65.00		110.00	
Circled Scroll						
Bowl, Master	175.00	150.00	125.00			
Bowl, Sauce	55.00	50.00	35.00			
Butter	475.00	350.00	300.00			
Creamer	175.00	170.00	125.00			
Cruet	700.00	675.00	465.00			
Jelly Compote	150.00	140.00	125.00			
Pitcher	475.00	425.00	400.00			
Tumbler	100.00	85.00	75.00			
Shakers, Pr.	325.00	300.00	250.00			
Spooner	175.00	170.00	125.00			
Sugar	250.00	225.00	200.00			
Cleopatra's Fan (Northwood Shell)						
Vase, Novelty, Rare	75.00	85.00				
Coin Dot Chevron Base						
Oil Lamp	300.00		225.00			
Coin Dot (Inverted Thumbprint Base)						
Lamp	300.00		200.00			
Coinspot* (Includes Variants – Prices Averaged)						
Barber Bottle	175.00	170.00	125.00		300.00	
Bowl, Master	50.00	40.00	30.00		70.00	
Bowl, Sauce	30.00	25.00	15.00		40.00	
Celery Vase	125.00	110.00	100.00	125.00	185.00	
Compote	65.00	45.00	35.00			
Cruet, Various	250.00	225.00	125.00	250.00	400.00	400.00 Rubina
Lamp (from syrup)	300.00		250.00		900.00	
Novelty Bowls	60.00	55.00	35.00			
Perfume	65.00	75.00	55.00			
Pickle Castor	300.00		225.00		750.00	
Pitcher	275.00	250.00	175.00	200.00	400.00	225.00 Rubina
Tumbler	40.00	35.00	25.00	35.00	100.00	90.00 Rubina

	Blue	Green	White	Vaseline/ Canary	Cranberry	Other
Shakers, Ea.	150.00	100.00	75.00	100.00	200.00	
Sugar Shaker	125.00	100.00	80.00	110.00	390.00	265.00 RUBINA
Syrup	175.00	155.00	150.00		400.00	325.00 RUBINA
Toothpick Holder	275.00	250.00	150.00	240.00	275.00	300.00 RUBINA
Tumble-Up	155.00	150.00	125.00		300.00	

Colonial Stairsteps

	Blue	Green	White	Vaseline/ Canary	Cranberry	Other
Creamer	100.00					
Sugar	100.00					
Toothpick Holder	200.00					

Commonwealth

	Blue	Green	White	Vaseline/ Canary	Cranberry	Other
Tumbler			25.00			

Compass

	Blue	Green	White	Vaseline/ Canary	Cranberry	Other
Plate, Rare	250.00	225.00				
Bowl, Scarce	150.00	150.00				

Concave Columns

	Blue	Green	White	Vaseline/ Canary	Cranberry	Other
Vase	100.00		75.00	100.00		
Vase Whimsey	125.00		100.00	125.00		

Conch & Twig

	Blue	Green	White	Vaseline/ Canary	Cranberry	Other
Wall-pocket Vase	250.00			250.00		

Consolidated Crisscross

	Blue	Green	White	Vaseline/ Canary	Cranberry	Other
Bowl, Master			125.00		200.00	
Bowl, Sauce			50.00		75.00	
Butter			450.00		725.00	
Celery Vase			150.00		175.00	
Creamer			250.00		375.00	
Cruet			275.00		800.00	
Finger Bowl			100.00		125.00	
Ivy Ball			300.00		700.00	
Mustard Pot			150.00		200.00	
Pitcher			600.00		950.00	
Tumbler			100.00		125.00	
Shakers, Ea.			100.00		100.00	175.00 Rubina
Spooner			225.00		300.00	
Sugar			350.00		400.00	
Sugar Shaker			325.00		550.00	600.00 Rubina
Syrup			325.00		825.00	725.00 Rubina
Toothpick Holder			200.00		500.00	

Constellation (Seafoam)

	Blue	Green	White	Vaseline/ Canary	Cranberry	Other
Compote	250.00		175.00			

Contessa

	Blue	Green	White	Vaseline/ Canary	Cranberry	Other
Basket, Hndl.	60.00			75.00		250.00 Amber
Breakfast Set, Ftd., 2 Pcs.	155.00					350.00 Amber
Pitcher	125.00					325.00 Amber

Coral

	Blue	Green	White	Vaseline/ Canary	Cranberry	Other
Bowl	50.00	40.00	25.00	45.00		

Coral Reef

	Blue	Green	White	Vaseline/ Canary	Cranberry	Other
Bitters Bottle	200.00		125.00		300.00	
Barber Bottle	200.00		125.00		300.00	
Finger Bowl	175.00		110.00		225.00	
Mini Nightlamp	500.00		400.00		1900.00	
Oil Lamp, Stemmed	450.00		335.00		1800.00	
Finger Lamp, Ftd.	425.00		325.00		1700.00	
Finger Lamp, Stemmed	500.00		400.00		2100.00	
Rose Bowl, Rare				750.00*		

	Blue	Green	White	Vaseline/ Canary	Cranberry	Other
Corn Vase *						
Fancy Vase, Scarce	225.00	300.00	145.00	200.00		
Cornith						
Vase, 8" – 13"	40.00		30.00			
Cornucopia						
Handled Vase	75.00		60.00			
Corolla						
Vase	225.00		175.00	200.00		
Coronation						
Creamer	45.00			40.00		
Sugar, Open	45.00			40.00		
Pitcher	200.00			200.00		
Tumbler	40.00			40.00		
Crocus						
Vase, Rare	350.00		250.00	350.00		
Crown Jewels						
Pitcher	200.00					
Tumbler	60.00					
Plate	100.00					
Platter	110.00					
Curtain Call						
Castor Set, Rare						550.00 Cobalt
Curtain Optic						
Guest Set, 2 Pcs.	125.00	100.00	80.00	125.00		
Pitcher, Various	225.00	210.00	150.00	200.00		
Tumbler, Various	50.00	45.00	35.00	45.00		
Cyclone						
Vase, v. Rare				800.00		
Daffodils						
Oil Lamp	325.00	300.00	225.00	300.00	350.00	
Pitcher	900.00	950.00	600.00	850.00	1350.00	
Tumbler, Rare	400.00	350.00	300.00	400.00	550.00	
Vase	300.00			265.00		
Add 25% for Goofus						
Dahlia Twist						
Epergne, Scarce	350.00	325.00	300.00			
Vase, Scarce	75.00	55.00	50.00			
Daisy Block						
Rowboat, 4 Sizes		100.00	75.00			
Daisy & Button						
Bowl, Novelty				65.00		
Bun Tray				150.00		
Lifeboat				85.00		
Daisy & Drape						
Vase, V. Rare				1500.00		
Daisy in Crisscross						
Pitcher	300.00				450.00	
Tumbler	60.00				100.00	
Syrup	275.00				475.00	
Daisy Dear						
Bowl, Rare	45.00	40.00	25.00			
Daisy & Fern *						
Barber Bottle					500.00	
Bowl, Master	80.00	100.00	55.00		250.00	

	Blue	Green	White	Vaseline/ Canary	Cranberry	Other
Bowl, Sauce	40.00	45.00	25.00		150.00	
Butter	225.00	250.00	175.00		300.00	
Creamer	75.00	90.00	60.00		425.00	
Cruet	200.00	175.00	150.00		525.00	
Mustard Pot	100.00	125.00	75.00		150.00	
Night Lamp	225.00	250.00	175.00		325.00	
Perfume	175.00	200.00	125.00		250.00	
Pickle Castor	325.00	325.00	250.00		450.00	
Pitcher, 3 Shapes	300.00	300.00	200.00		300.00 – 750.00	
Tumbler	50.00	50.00	25.00		100.00	
Rose Bowl					125.00	
Shakers, Pr.	300.00	275.00	175.00		300.00	
Spooner	75.00	100.00	55.00		425.00	
Sugar	100.00	125.00	75.00		250.00	
Sugar Shaker	200.00	225.00	175.00		275.00	
Syrup, Various, avg.	250.00	225.00	200.00		250.00 – 550.00	
Toothpick Holder	160.00	175.00	125.00		225.00	
Vase	150.00	150.00	100.00		200.00	

Daisy & Greek Key

	Blue	Green	White	Vaseline/ Canary	Cranberry	Other
Sauce, Ftd.	75.00	60.00	35.00			

Daisy Intaglio

	Blue	Green	White	Vaseline/ Canary	Cranberry	Other
Basket		185.00	155.00			
Bowl		100.00	90.00			
Plate		135.00	110.00			

Daisy May (Leaf Rays)

	Blue	Green	White	Vaseline/ Canary	Cranberry	Other
Nappy or Bon-Bon	45.00	50.00	25.00			

Daisy & Plume

	Blue	Green	White	Vaseline/ Canary	Cranberry	Other
Bowl Ftd.	50.00	45.00	30.00			
Rose Bowl, Ftd.	60.00	55.00	35.00			

Daisy Wreath

	Blue	Green	White	Vaseline/ Canary	Cranberry	Other
Bowl, Rare	165.00					

Dandelion

	Blue	Green	White	Vaseline/ Canary	Cranberry	Other
Mug, V. Rare	1,200.00					

Davidson Epergne

	Blue	Green	White	Vaseline/ Canary	Cranberry	Other
Epergne, 14"	300.00			300.00		

Davidson Shell

	Blue	Green	White	Vaseline/ Canary	Cranberry	Other
Spill Vase	125.00			125.00		

Desert Garden

	Blue	Green	White	Vaseline/ Canary	Cranberry	Other
Bowl	45.00	40.00	25.00			

Diamond & Daisy

	Blue	Green	White	Vaseline/ Canary	Cranberry	Other
Basket, Hndl.	100.00	110.00	55.00			
Bowl Novelty	60.00	70.00	35.00			

Diamond Maple Leaf

	Blue	Green	White	Vaseline/ Canary	Cranberry	Other
Bowl, Hndl.	75.00	70.00	45.00			
Novelty, Hndl.	40.00	50.00	25.00	50.00		
(add 10% for signed Pcs.)						

Diamond Optic

	Blue	Green	White	Vaseline/ Canary	Cranberry	Other
Compote	50.00		40.00			
Stemmed Cardtray	60.00		50.00			

Diamond & Oval Thumbprint

	Blue	Green	White	Vaseline/ Canary	Cranberry	Other
Vase	40.00	45.00	25.00			

Diamond Point

	Blue	Green	White	Vaseline/ Canary	Cranberry	Other
Vase	40.00	50.00	30.00			

	Blue	Green	White	Vaseline/ Canary	Cranberry	Other
Diamond Point Columns						
Vase, Scarce	200.00	175.00	75.00			
Diamond Point & Fleur de Lis						
Bowl, Novelty	50.00	55.00	40.00			
Nut Bowl		65.00				
Diamond Spearhead						
Bowl, Master	180.00	185.00	125.00	180.00		140.00*
Bowl, Sauce	55.00	60.00	35.00	45.00		40.00*
Butter	500.00	575.00	400.00	500.00		475.00*
Celery Vase	250.00	250.00	150.00	250.00		250.00*
Creamer	200.00	225.00	150.00	200.00		200.00*
Cup & Saucer Set				250.00		
Goblet	175.00	150.00	100.00	150.00		135.00*
Jelly Compote	200.00	150.00	125.00	175.00		200.00*
Mini Creamer	200.00	200.00	125.00	200.00		225.00 Sapphire
Mug	180.00	200.00	100.00	150.00		175.00*
Oil Bottle	125.00			100.00		100.00
Pitcher	725.00	625.00	400.00	500.00		625.00*
Tumbler	125.00	100.00	60.00	90.00		100.00*
Shakers, Pr.	150.00	175.00	130.00	175.00		175.00*
Spittoon Whimsey		55.00		500.00		
Spooner	175.00	200.00	150.00	175.00		175.00*
Sugar	250.00	225.00	175.00	250.00		250.00*
Syrup	650.00	700.00	550.00	625.00		750.00*
Tall Creamer	200.00			200.00		275.00
Tall Compote	400.00	400.00	300.00	400.00		450.00
Toothpick Holder	150.00	125.00	100.00	125.00		150.00
Water Carafe	250.00		175.00	225.00		
*Emerald or Sapphire						
Diamond Stem						
Vase, 3 Sizes, Rare	175.00	200.00	100.00	175.00		125.00 Aqua
Vase, JIP Shape, Rare	225.00	225.00	150.00	225.00		
Diamond Wave						
Pitcher w/lid					175.00	250.00 Amethyst
Tumbler					50.00	
Vase, 5"					85.00	
Diamonds						
Cruet					350.00	
Pitcher, 2 Shapes					400.00	275.00 Rubina
Vase, 6", Decorated			75.00			
Dogwood Drape (Palm Rosette)						
Compote	150.00		120.00			
Plate, Rare	125.00		90.00			
Dolly Madison						
Bowl, Master	60.00	70.00	50.00			
Bowl, Novelty	60.00	70.00	45.00			
Bowl, Sauce	30.00	35.00	20.00			
Butter	325.00	350.00	250.00			
Creamer	90.00	100.00	70.00			
Pitcher	400.00	425.00	300.00			
Tumbler	80.00	95.00	50.00			
Spooner	80.00	90.00	50.00			
Sugar	150.00	160.00	100.00			
Plate, 6", Scarce	110.00	110.00	65.00			

	Blue	Green	White	Vaseline/ Canary	Cranberry	Other
Dolphin*						
Compote, Scarce	85.00		50.00	75.00		
Dolphin & Herons						
Compote, Ftd., Novelty	495.00		280.00	425.00		
Tray, Ftd., Novelty	490.00		275.00		800.00	
Dolphin Petticoat						
Candlesticks, Pr.	175.00		125.00	165.00		
Double Dolphin (1533)						
Compote, Rare	150.00		100.00			
Double Greek Key						
Bowl, Master	75.00		60.00			
Bowl, Sauce	40.00		25.00			
Butter	325.00		250.00			
Celery Vase	175.00		125.00			
Creamer	100.00		75.00			
Mustard Pot	200.00		150.00			
Pickle Tray	150.00		90.00			
Pitcher	400.00		325.00			
Tumbler	90.00		60.00			
Shakers, Pr.	250.00		175.00			
Spooner	110.00		70.00			
Sugar	200.00		125.00			
Toothpick Holder	250.00		200.00			
Double Stemmed Rose						
Bowl, V. Rare	275.00	225.00	175.00			
Dragon & Lotus						
Bowl, Rare			325.00			
Dragon Lady						
Rose Bowl	160.00	150.00	90.00			
Novelty Bowl	140.00	130.00	90.00			
Vase	100.00	100.00	60.00			
Drapery, Northwood's						
Bowl, Master	110.00		75.00			
Bowl, Sauce	40.00		25.00			
Butter	200.00		175.00			
Creamer	10.00		80.00			
Pitcher	250.00		225.00			
Tumbler	75.00		50.00			
Rose Bowl	100.00		75.00			
Spooner	85.00		70.00			
Sugar	145.00		125.00			
Vase	175.00	200.00	155.00	175.00		
Duchess						
Bowl, Master	95.00		65.00	80.00		
Bowl, Sauce	35.00		25.00	35.00		
Butter	200.00		150.00	175.00		
Creamer	65.00		45.00	65.00		
Cruet	225.00		175.00	200.00		
Lampshade	100.00		75.00			
Pitcher	200.00		165.00	185.00		
Tumbler	40.00		25.00	35.00		
Spooner	70.00		50.00	70.00		
Sugar	110.00		75.00	110.00		
Toothpick Holder	165.00		125.00	150.00		

	Blue	Green	White	Vaseline/ Canary	Cranberry	Other
Dugan Intaglio Grape						
Plate, 12½", Rare			250.00			
Bowl			125.00			
Compote			85.00			
Dugan Jack-in-the-Pulpit						
Vase, 4½"	50.00	50.00	35.00			
Vase, Hex Base, 7½"	60.00	70.00	40.00			
(Floral etched-add 15%)						
Dugan Peach Intaglio						
Plate, 13"			185.00			
Bowl			100.00			
Compote			100.00			
Dugan's Honeycomb						
Bowl, Various Shapes, Rare	175.00	175.00	150.00	200.00		
Dugan's #1013 (Wide Rib)						
Vase	65.00	75.00	50.00			
Bowl, Whimsey	50.00	55.00	40.00			
Plate	70.00	80.00	60.00			
Dugan's Olive Nappy						
One Shape	45.00	40.00	25.00			
Dugan Strawberry Intaglio						
Bowl, 9"			45.00			
Fruit Bowl, Stemmed			65.00			
Ellen						
Vase	50.00	55.00	35.00			
Ellipse & Diamond						
Pitcher					500.00	
Tumbler					115.00	
Elson Dew Drop						
Butter, Covered			75.00			
Creamer or Spooner			35.00			
Sugar w/lid			40.00			
Berry Bowl, Lg.			40.00			
Berry Bowl, Sm.			15.00			
Mug			50.00			
Breakfast Set, 2 Pcs.			80.00			
Celery Vase			65.00			
English Drape						
Vase	60.00		35.00	65.00		
English Duck						
Novelty Dish	150.00			150.00		
English Salt Dip						
One Shape			75.00			
English Spool						
Vase	75.00			70.00		
Estate		65.00	85.00	45.00		
Vase, Scarce						
Everglades						
Bowl, Oval, Master	200.00			200.00		
Bowl, Oval, Sauce	45.00			50.00		
Butter	375.00			390.00		
Creamer	150.00			150.00		
Cruet	475.00			500.00		
Jelly Compote	150.00			150.00		

	Blue	Green	White	Vaseline/ Canary	Cranberry	Other
Pitcher	500.00			500.00		
Tumbler	100.00			100.00		
Shakers, Pr.	275.00			300.00		
Spooner	150.00			150.00		
Sugar	200.00			210.00		
Everglades (Cambridge)						
Compote			75.00			
Fan						
Bowl, Master	75.00	70.00	65.00			
Bowl, Sauce	30.00	30.00	20.00			
Butter	400.00	400.00	200.00			
Creamer	125.00	120.00	75.00			
Gravy Boat	50.00	50.00	35.00			
Novelty Bowls	40.00	40.00	25.00			
Pitcher	300.00	300.00	200.00			
Tumbler	40.00	30.00	20.00			
Spooner	125.00	110.00	85.00			
Sugar	200.00	200.00	150.00			
Whimsey Bowls	55.00	55.00	35.00			
Fancy Fantails						
Bowl	40.00	45.00	25.00	40.00		
Rose Bowl	45.00	50.00	30.00	45.00		
Add 10% for frit						
Feathers						
Vase	35.00	30.00	25.00			
Whimsey Bowl, Rare			125.00			
Whimsey Nut Bowl, Rare	150.00	150.00				
Fenton #100						
Bowl				50.00		60.00 Amethyst
Fenton #220 (Stripe)						
Pitcher w/Lid	250.00	250.00	175.00	225.00		
Tumbler, Hndl.	30.00	35.00	20.00	30.00		
Tumble-up, Complete	150.00	150.00	100.00	145.00		
Fenton's #260						
Compote, Tall	50.00		35.00	50.00		
Fenton #370						
Bowl						45.00 Amber
Vase						50.00 Amber
Nappy						55.00 Amber
Bon-Bon						50.00 Amber
Fenton #950						
Cornucopia Candlestick, ea.						95.00 Amethyst
Fenton Drapery						
Pitcher	450.00	425.00	275.00			
Tumbler	75.00	65.00	40.00			
Fern						
Barber Bottle	150.00		100.00		300.00	
Bowl, Master	100.00		80.00		125.00	
Bowl, Sauce	50.00		40.00		55.00	
Butter	275.00		225.00		400.00	
Celery Vase	125.00		100.00		150.00	
Creamer	125.00		100.00		150.00	
Cruet	225.00		225.00		500.00	
Finger Bowl	75.00		50.00		100.00	
Mustard Pot	150.00		125.00		175.00	

	Blue	Green	White	Vaseline/Canary	Cranberry	Other
Pitcher, Various	275.00		200.00		750.00	
Tumbler	50.00		50.00		110.00	
Shakers, Pr.	175.00		100.00		165.00	
Spooner	125.00		100.00		150.00	
Sugar	200.00		175.00		250.00	
Sugar Shaker, Various	125.00		100.00		550.00	
Syrup	275.00		220.00		600.00	
Toothpick Holder, Rare	350.00		200.00		475.00	
Fine Rib (Fenton)						
Vase, V. Rare				500.00		
Finecut & Roses						
Novelty Bowls	45.00	50.00	40.00			
Rose Bowl, Rare	65.00	75.00	50.00			
Fish in the Sea						
Vase, Scarce	400.00	425.00	300.00	600.00		
Vase Whimsey, Scarce	295.00	390.00	270.00			
Fishnet						
Epergne	175.00		145.00			
(One Shape, 2 Pcs.)						
Fishscale & Beads						
Bowl	50.00		30.00			
Flora						
Bowl, Master	100.00		80.00	100.00		
Bowl, Sauce	50.00		30.00	40.00		
Butter	300.00		200.00	265.00		
Celery Vase	130.00		100.00	110.00		
Creamer	100.00		80.00	100.00		
Cruet	750.00		450.00	600.00		
Jelly Compote	150.00		110.00	150.00		
Novelty Bowl	70.00		45.00	60.00		
Pitcher	500.00		410.00	480.00		
Tumbler	90.00		65.00	85.00		
Shakers, Pr.	400.00		300.00	400.00		
Spooner	110.00		300.00	375.00		
Sugar	145.00		100.00	125.00		
Syrup	410.00		300.00	400.00		
Toothpick Holder	480.00		300.00	400.00		
Floral Eyelet*						
Pitcher	525.00		400.00		850.00	
Tumbler	100.00		100.00		250.00	
Fluted Bars & Beads						
Novelty Bowl	60.00	55.00	50.00	70.00		
Rose Bowl	55.00	50.00	45.00	65.00		
Vase Whimsey	65.00	60.00	55.00	75.00		
Fluted Scrolls (Klondyke)						
Bowl, Master	85.00		60.00	75.00		
Bowl, Sauce	40.00		30.00	35.00		
Butter	185.00		165.00	175.00		
Creamer	80.00		55.00	70.00		
Cruet	200.00		175.00	185.00		
Epergne, Sm.	125.00		100.00	125.00		
Novelty Bowl	55.00		40.00	55.00		
Puff Box	75.00		50.00	75.00		
Pitcher	250.00		175.00	200.00		
Tumbler	100.00		50.00	75.00		

	Blue	Green	White	Vaseline/ Canary	Cranberry	Other
Rose Bowl	150.00		100.00	125.00		
Shakers, Pr.	100.00		75.00	85.00		
Spooner	80.00		55.00	60.00		
Sugar	140.00		100.00	110.00		

NOTE: Fluted Scroll with Flower Band is priced the same as above.

	Blue	Green	White	Vaseline/ Canary	Cranberry	Other
Fluted Scroll with Vine						
Vase, Ftd.	100.00		50.00	110.00		
Forked Stripe						
Barber Bottle			275.00			
Four Pillars						
Vase	75.00	70.00	40.00	75.00		
Frosted Leaf & Basketweave						
Butter	275.00		200.00	250.00		
Creamer	150.00		130.00	135.00		
Spooner	150.00		125.00	135.00		
Sugar	175.00		150.00	165.00		
Vase Whimsey	150.00		125.00	140.00		
Garland of Roses						
Stemmed Tray, rare			250.00			
Gonderman (Adonis) Hob						
Cruet						425.00 Amber
Gonderman (Adonis) Swirl						
Bowl, Master	100.00					100.00 Amber
Bowl, Sauce	50.00					50.00 Amber
Butter	400.00					350.00 Amber
Celery Vase	225.00					200.00 Amber
Creamer	175.00					125.00 Amber
Cruet	400.00					385.00 Amber
Pitcher	400.00					400.00 Amber
Tumbler	100.00					90.00 Amber
Shade	125.00					100.00 Amber
Spooner	150.00					125.00 Amber
Sugar	250.00					225.00 Amber
Syrup	400.00					375.00 Amber
Toothpick Holder	300.00					200.00 Amber
Gossamer Threads						
Bowl	50.00					
Finger Bowl	55.00					
Plate, 6"	70.00					
Grape & Cable						
Bon-Bon				450.00		
Centerpiece Bowl	300.00	300.00	225.00	265.00		
Fruit Bowl, Lg.	300.00	300.00	245.00	275.00		
Grape & Cherry						
Bowl	75.00	90.00	50.00	80.00		
Grapevine Cluster						
Vase, Ftd.	175.00		125.00	165.00		200.00 Aqua
Grecian Urn						
Vase, 4½"	65.00					
Greek Key & Ribs						
Bowl	65.00	55.00	35.00			
Greek Key & Scales						
Novelty Bowl	90.00	80.00	50.00			

	Blue	Green	White	Vaseline/Canary	Cranberry	Other
Harrow						
Creamer	75.00			70.00		
Sugar, Open	70.00			65.00		
Wine, Stemmed	40.00			40.00		
Cordial, Stemmed	35.00			35.00		
Heart-Handle Open O's						
Ring Tray	100.00	90.00	75.00			
Hearts & Clubs						
Bowl, Ftd.	60.00	55.00	35.00			
Hearts & Flowers						
Bowl	150.00		100.00			
Compote	350.00		300.00			
Heatherbloom						
Vase	40.00	30.00	20.00			
Herringbone						
Cruet	300.00		225.00		700.00	
Pitcher	575.00		475.00		725.00	
Tumbler	100.00		65.00		150.00	
Heron & Peacock*						
Mug	75.00		65.00			
Hilltop Vines						
Novelty Chalice	65.00	60.00	40.00			
Hobnail & Panelled Thumbprint						
Pitcher	300.00		150.00	300.00		
Tumbler	75.00		45.00	75.00		
Butter	200.00		145.00	175.00		
Sugar	125.00		100.00	90.00		
Creamer	85.00		60.00	75.00		
Spooner	85.00		65.00	75.00		
Bowl, Master	75.00		60.00	65.00		
Bowl, Sauce	35.00		25.00	30.00		
Hobnail, Hobbs						
Barber Bottle	150.00		125.00	145.00		
Bowl, Master, Sq.	100.00		80.00	100.00		
Bowl, Sauce, Sq.	40.00		30.00	50.00		
Bride's Basket	450.00			425.00	525.00	500.00 Rubina
Butter	300.00		200.00	225.00		
Celery Vase	175.00		125.00	145.00		225.00 Rubina
Creamer	100.00		100.00	125.00		
Cruet	200.00		200.00	190.00		
Finger Bowl	65.00		50.00	55.00		
Lemonade Set, Complete	625.00				725.00	
Pitcher, 5 Sizes	200 – 400.00		150 – 250.00	175 – 325.00	300.00 – 600.00	250.00 – 450.00 Rubina
Tumbler	75.00		50.00	75.00		125.00 Rubina
Shakers, Ea.			200.00		400.00	
Spooner	10.00		100.00	125.00		
Sugar	200.00		135.00	175.00		
Syrup	225.00		200.00	200.00		
Water Tray						
Hobnail, Northwood's						
Bowl, Master	55.00					
Bowl, Sauce	30.00					
Breakfast Set, 2 Pcs.	150.00					

	Blue	Green	White	Vaseline/ Canary	Cranberry	Other
Butter	150.00					
Celery Vase	100.00					
Creamer	65.00					
Mug	100.00					
Pitcher	150.00					
Tumbler	50.00					
Spooner	75.00					
Sugar	125.00					
Hobnail 4-Footed						
Butter			155.00	175.00		225.00 Cobalt
Creamer			70.00	90.00		100.00 Cobalt
Spooner			70.00	85.00		100.00 Cobalt
Sugar			80.00	125.00		150.00 Cobalt
Hobnail in Square* (vesta)						
Barber Bottle			120.00			
Bowl, Master			75.00			
Bowl, Sauce			25.00			
Bowl w/stand	150.00					
Butter			200.00			
Celery Vase			145.00			
Compote, Various			100.00			
Creamer			100.00			
Pitcher			245.00			
Tumbler			50.00			
Shaker's Pr.			100.00			
Spooner			100.00			
Sugar			150.00			
Holly						
Bowl			175.00			
Holly & Berry						
Nappy, Rare			275.00			
Honeycomb						
Vase	75.00	100.00	45.00			
Honeycomb (Blown)						
Barber Bottle	175.00		125.00		175.00	200.00 Amber
Cracker Jar	325.00		250.00		400.00	425.00 Amber
Pitcher	325.00		225.00		500.00	450.00 Amber
Tumbler	80.00		50.00		100.00	75.00 Amber
Syrup	300.00		275.00		425.00	450.00 Amber
Honeycomb & Clover						
Bowl, Master	100.00	75.00	50.00			
Bowl, Sauce	50.00	35.00	25.00			
Bowl, Novelty	75.00	75.00	50.00			
Butter	400.00	350.00	250.00			
Creamer	150.00	140.00	125.00			
Pitcher	400.00	350.00	285.00			
Tumbler	100.00	80.00	55.00			
Spooner	150.00	150.00	100.00			
Sugar	300.00	275.00	150.00			
Horse Chestnut						
Blown Vase				100.00		
Idyll						
Bowl, Master	60.00	60.00	45.00			
Bowl, Sauce	30.00	30.00	25.00			

	Blue	Green	White	Vaseline/ Canary	Cranberry	Other
Bowl, 6" – 7"	40.00	45.00	30.00			
Butter	350.00	375.00	300.00			
Creamer	150.00	125.00	75.00			
Cruet	225.00	200.00	175.00			
Pitcher	375.00	375.00	300.00			
Tumbler	100.00	90.00	70.00			
Shakers, Pr.	125.00	115.00	100.00			
Spooner	150.00	125.00	75.00			
Sugar	175.00	200.00	150.00			
Toothpick Holder	400.00	325.00	275.00			
Tray	125.00	110.00	100.00			
Inside Ribbing						
Bowl, Master	70.00		40.00	75.00		
Bowl, Sauce	30.00		20.00	35.00		
Butter	225.00		150.00	250.00		
Celery Vase	60.00		35.00	60.00		
Creamer	75.00		55.00	80.00		
Cruet	150.00		100.00	150.00		
Jelly Compote	75.00		30.00	65.00		
Pitcher	300.00		160.00	300.00		
Tumbler	65.00		30.00	70.00		
Rose Bowl	80.00					
Shakers, Pr.	125.00		75.00	100.00		
Spooner	75.00		60.00	80.00		
Sugar	125.00		100.00	125.00		
Syrup	155.00		100.00	150.00		
Toothpick Holder	200.00		175.00	200.00		
Tray	55.00		30.00	50.00		
Intaglio						
Bowl, Master, Ftd.	225.00		100.00	250.00		
Bowl, Sauce, Std.	35.00		25.00	50.00		
Butter	500.00		275.00			
Creamer	100.00		50.00			
Cruet	200.00		150.00	300.00		
Jelly Compote	60.00		45.00	80.00		
Novelty Bowl	50.00		30.00	65.00		
Pitcher	250.00		150.00			
Tumbler	110.00		65.00			
Shakers, Pr.	100.00		75.00			
Spooner	100.00		60.00			
Sugar	175.00		100.00			
Intaglio, Dugan						
Bowl, 7" – 10"			120.00			
Compote, 5" – 7"			100.00			
Compote, 8" – 11"			150.00			
Nappy, 6" – 9"			75.00			
Plate, 11"			135.00			
Interior Panel						
Fan Vase	55.00	50.00	30.00	55.00		100.00 Amethyst
Interior Poinsettia						
Tumbler	50.00	65.00	40.00			
Interior Swirl						
Rose Bowl	100.00		60.00	100.00		

	Blue	Green	White	Vaseline/ Canary	Cranberry	Other
Inverted Chevron						
Vase	75.00	65.00	45.00			
Inverted Coindot						
Rose Bowl			55.00	100.00		
Tumbler		60.00	35.00			
Inverted Fan & Feather*						
Bowl, Master	300.00		375.00		200.00	
Bowl, Sauce	100.00	100.00		40.00		
Butter	500.00		400.00			
Card Tray Whimsey	225.00	250.00	175.00	250.00		
Creamer	225.00		175.00			
Cruet, Rare	500.00					
Jelly Compote, Rare	250.00		175.00			
Novelty Bowl, v. Rare		250.00		300.00		
Pitcher	750.00		625.00			
Tumbler	100.00		75.00			
Plate, V. Rare				500.00		
Punch Bowl, Rare	850.00					
Punch Cup, Rare	50.00					
Rose Bowl	225.00	300.00		175.00		
Rose Bowl Whimsey	250.00	275.00	225.00	250.00		
Shakers, Pr.	375.00					
Spittoon Whimsey	350.00		275.00	350.00		
Spooner	225.00		175.00			
Sugar	300.00		250.00			
Toothpick, Rare	500.00					
Vase Whimsey, Rare	200.00	200.00	150.00			
Iris with Meander						
Bowl, Master	200.00	150.00	75.00	155.00		
Bowl, Sauce, 2 Sizes	50.00	35.00	20.00	40.00		
Butter	300.00	275.00	225.00	275.00		
Creamer	100.00	80.00	60.00	75.00		
Cruet	500.00	400.00	275.00	400.00		
Jelly Compote	55.00	50.00	35.00	45.00		
Pitcher	400.00	375.00	275.00	325.00		
Tumbler	80.00	75.00	55.00	75.00		
Pickle Dish	85.00	75.00	55.00	75.00		
Plate	100.00	85.00	60.00	80.00		
Shakers, Pr.	225.00	200.00	175.00	200.00		
Spooner	100.00	80.00	55.00	75.00		
Sugar	175.00	150.00	100.00	175.00		
Toothpick Holder	150.00	125.00	75.00	125.00		
Vase, Tall	60.00	55.00	35.00	60.00		
Jackson						
Bowl, Master	100.00		75.00	80.00		
Bowl, Sauce	35.00		20.00	35.00		
Butter	225.00		150.00	225.00		
Candy Dish	55.00		35.00	55.00		
Creamer	80.00		60.00	75.00		
Cruet	200.00		175.00	200.00		
Epergne, Sm.	175.00		100.00	150.00		
Powder Jar	75.00		45.00	70.00		
Pitcher	500.00		400.00	450.00		
Tumbler	80.00		65.00	85.00		

	Blue	Green	White	Vaseline/ Canary	Cranberry	Other
Spooner	80.00		65.00	75.00		
Sugar	125.00		100.00	125.00		
Jazz						
Vase	50.00	55.00	30.00			
Jefferson #270						
Master Bowl	100.00	85.00	55.00			
Sauce	45.00	45.00	25.00			
Jefferson Shield						
Bowl, V. Rare	300.00	350.00	200.00			
Jefferson Spool						
Vase	5.00	45.00	40.00			
Vase Whimsey	55.00	50.00	45.00			
Jefferson Stripe						
Vase, J.I.P.	60.00	65.00	40.00			
Jefferson Wheel						
Bowl	55.00	50.00	45.00			
Jester						
Epergne	350.00	375.00	290.00	350.00		
Jewel & Fan						
Banana Bowl	125.00	145.00	100.00	140.00		135.00 Emerald Gr.
Bowl	60.00	55.00	40.00	75.00		
Jewel & Flower						
Bowl, Master	75.00		50.00	75.00		
Bowl, Sauce	35.00		25.00	40.00		
Butter	400.00		225.00	325.00		
Creamer	125.00		100.00	150.00		
Cruet	700.00		325.00	645.00		
Novelty Bowl	55.00		30.00	55.00		
Pitcher	675.00		325.00	500.00		
Tumbler	100.00		65.00	80.00		
Shakers, Pr.	175.00		125.00	165.00		
Spooner	125.00		100.00	125.00		
Sugar	200.00		125.00	200.00		
Jewelled Heart						
Bowl, Master	65.00	60.00	50.00			
Bowl, Sauce	30.00	25.00	20.00			
Butter	325.00	300.00	225.00			
Condiment Set						
(4 Pcs., Complete)	1000.00	1000.00	750.00			
Compote	150.00	150.00	100.00			
Creamer	175.00	150.00	100.00			
Cruet	400.00	400.00	310.00			
Novelty Bowl	50.00	40.00	30.00			
Pitcher	400.00	300.00	200.00			
Tumbler	100.00	65.00	40.00			
Plate, Sm.	75.00	70.00	55.00			
Shakers, Pr.	350.00	350.00	275.00			
Spooner	175.00	150.00	100.00			
Sugar	200.00	195.00	125.00			
Sugar Shaker	350.00	350.00	275.00			
Syrup	500.00	475.00	400.00			
Toothpick Holder	250.00	250.00	200.00			
Tray	250.00	225.00	200.00			

	Blue	Green	White	Vaseline/ Canary	Cranberry	Other
Jewels & Drapery						
Novelty Bowl	55.00	50.00	35.00			70.00 Aqua
Vase (from bowl)	50.00	45.00	30.00			75.00 Aqua
Jolly Bear						
Bowl, V. Rare	350.00	325.00	200.00			
Keyhole						
Bowl, Scarce	85.00	90.00	60.00			
Rose Bowl	175.00	175.00	150.00			
King Richard						
Compote	200.00		150.00	225.00		
Kitten's (Fenton)						
Cup, V. Rare						550.00 Amethyst
Saucer, V. Rare						450.00 Amethyst
Lady Caroline						
Basket	60.00			60.00		
Creamer	60.00			60.00		
Sugar, 2 Shapes	55.00			55.00		
Whimsey, 3 Hndl.	75.00			70.00		
Spill	65.00			65.00		
Lady Chippendale						
Compote, Tall						100.00 Cobalt
Late Coinspot						
Pitcher	150.00	150.00	110.00			
Tumbler	45.00	35.00	25.00			
Lattice & Daisy						
Tumbler, Scarce	90.00		65.00	125.00		
Lattice Medallions						
Bowl	55.00	50.00	40.00			
Lattice & Points						
Bowl, Novelty			55.00			
Hat Shape			60.00			
Vase			75.00			
Laura (Single Flower Framed)						
Bowl, Scarce	55.00	50.00	35.00			
Nappy, Scarce	60.00	55.00	35.00			
Plate, Ruffled, Rare	150.00	150.00	125.00			
Laurel Swag & Bows						
Shade, Gas						125.00 Amethyst
Leaf & Beads						
Bowl, Ftd. or Dome	60.00	55.00	35.00			
Bowl, Whimsey	70.00	60.00	40.00			
Rose Bowl	75.00	70.00	45.00			
Leaf Chalice						
Novelty Compote (found in several shapes from same mould)	100.00	125.00	65.00	100.00		175.00 Cobalt
Leaf & Diamonds						
Bowl	50.00	65.00	30.00			
Leaf & Leaflets (Long Leaf)						
Bowl	60.00		45.00			
Leaf Mold						
Bowl, Master					140.00	
Bowl, Sauce					55.00	
Butter					425.00	

	Blue	Green	White	Vaseline/ Canary	Cranberry	Other
Celery Vase					325.00	
Creamer					175.00	
Cruet					650.00	
Pitcher					550.00	
Tumbler					100.00	
Shakers, Pr.					550.00	
Spooner					175.00	
Sugar					300.00	
Sugar Shaker					350.00	
Syrup					375.00	
Toothpick Holder					500.00	
Leaf Rosette & Beads						
Bowl, Low, V. Scarce	250.00	260.00	175.00			
Lily Pool						
Epergne	300.00		250.00	300.00		
Lined Heart						
Vase	40.00	40.00	30.00			
Linking Rings						
Bowl	60.00			65.00		
Pitcher	125.00			125.00		
Juice Glass	40.00			45.00		
Compote	75.00			85.00		
Tray	80.00			90.00		
Little Nell						
Vase	40.00	35.00	20.00			
Little Swan* (Pastel Swan)						
Novelty, 2 Sizes	100.00	100.00	50.00	90.00		
Lords & Ladies						
Butter	100.00			125.00		
Creamer	70.00			85.00		
Open Sugar	75.00			90.00		
Plate, 7½"	100.00			125.00		
Lorna						
Vase	40.00		30.00	45.00		
Lotus						
Bowl w/underplate	160.00		140.00	160.00		
Lustre Flute						
Bowl, Master	275.00	350.00	225.00			
Bowl, Sauce	50.00		35.00			
Butter	500.00		300.00			
Creamer	150.00		125.00			
Custard Cup	50.00		30.00			
Pitcher	400.00		325.00			
Tumbler	100.00		65.00			
Spooner	150.00		125.00			
Sugar	275.00		200.00			
Vase	75.00		50.00			
Many Loops						
Bowl, Ruffled	50.00	45.00	35.00			
Bowl, Deep Round	60.00	55.00	40.00			
Rose Bowl, Scarce	75.00	70.00	45.00			
Many Ribs (Model Flint)						
Vase	65.00		35.00	50.00		

	Blue	Green	White	Vaseline/Canary	Cranberry	Other
Maple Leaf						
Jelly Compote	110.00	100.00	70.00	200.00		
Maple Leaf Chalice						
One Shape	75.00	85.00	50.00	65.00		
Markham Swirl Band						
Oil Lamp	275.00		250.00	275.00	550.00	
Mary Ann						
Vase, Rare	300.00		275.00			
May Basket						
Basket Shape	80.00	75.00	60.00	100.00		
Meander						
Bowl	60.00	55.00	35.00			
Melon Optic Swirl						
Bowl, Rare	80.00	90.00	60.00	85.00		
Melon Swirl						
Pitcher	450.00					
Tumbler	75.00					
Milky Way (Country Kitchen Vt.)						
Bowl, Rare			300.00			
Miniature Epergne						
Epergne, 1 Lily	150.00			150.00		
Monkey (Under a Tree)						
Pitcher, Rare			1000.00			
Tumbler, Rare			500.00			
Mug, V. Rare			600.00			
National Swirl						
Pitcher	275.00	275.00				
Tumbler	50.00	50.00				
National's # 17						
Bouquet Vase, 8"	150.00	150.00		150.00		
Nesting Robin						
Bowl			300.00			
Netted Cherries						
Bowl			45.00			
Plate			65.00			
Netted Roses						
Bowl	70.00	90.00	50.00			
Plate	120.00	130.00	100.00			
New England Pineapple						
Goblet, Rare			60.00			
Northern Star						
Banana Bowl	75.00	70.00	50.00			
Bowl	65.00	60.00	40.00			
Plate	100.00	100.00	50.00			
Northwood Block						
Celery Vase	60.00	60.00	40.00	55.00		
Novelty Bowl	50.00	45.00	30.00	45.00		
Northwood's Many Ribs						
Vase	70.00	65.00	50.00	65.00		
Northwood's Poppy						
Pickle Dish, V. Rare	300.00					
Ocean Shell						
Novelty, Ftd., 3 Variations	85.00	90.00	55.00			

	Blue	Green	White	Vaseline/ Canary	Cranberry	Other
Old Man Winter						
Basket, Sm.	75.00	100.00	60.00			
Basket, Lg., Ftd.	150.00	175.00	100.00	275.00		
Opal Loops						
Vase			110.00			
Decanter			160.00			
Flask			195.00			
Glass Pipe			180.00			
Opal Open* (Beaded Panels)						
Bowl, Novelty	50.00	55.00	30.00	50.00		
Ring Bowl, Hndl.	100.00	90.00	55.00	85.00		
Rose Bowl, Novelty	50.00	60.00	30.00	50.00		
Vase, Novelty	40.00	40.00	25.00	40.00		
Opal Spiral						
Tumbler	350.00					
Sugar	100.00					
Opal Urn						
Vase	80.00		50.00	80.00		
Open O's						
Bowl, Novelty	55.00	50.00	25.00	45.00		
Spittoon Whimsey	125.00	100.00	75.00	100.00		
Rose Bowl Whimsey	100.00	90.00	55.00	85.00		
Optic Basket						
One Shape				150.00		
Optic Panel						
Vase JIP				100.00		
Orange Tree						
Mug, Rare						250.00 Cstrd. Opal
Overlapping Leaves (Leaf Tiers)						
Bowl, Ftd.	175.00	175.00	150.00			
Plate, Ftd.	250.00	275.00	195.00			
Rose Bowl, Ftd.	175.00	185.00	150.00			
Over-All Hob						
Bowl, Master	75.00		40.00	70.00		
Bowl, Sauce	30.00		20.00	25.00		
Butter	250.00		175.00	225.00		
Celery Vase	75.00		50.00	75.00		
Creamer	100.00		50.00	90.00		
Finger Bowl	60.00		30.00	60.00		
Mug	75.00		55.00	75.00		
Pitcher	225.00		165.00	200.00		
Tumbler	65.00		25.00	50.00		
Spooner	100.00		50.00	90.00		
Sugar	175.00		100.00	150.00		
Toothpick Holder	200.00		135.00	200.00		
Palisades (Lined Lattice)						
Bowl, Novelty	45.00	50.00	35.00	55.00		
Vase, Novelty	50.00	45.00	35.00	50.00		
Palm & Scroll						
Bowl, Ftd.	65.00	60.00	40.00	60.00		
Rose Bowl, Ftd.	75.00	70.00	50.00	70.00		
Palm Beach						
Bowl, Master	85.00			85.00		

	Blue	Green	White	Vaseline/ Canary	Cranberry	Other
Bowl, Sauce, 2 Sizes	40.00			50.00		
Butter	300.00			300.00		
Card Tray Whimsey, Rare				500.00		
Creamer	150.00			140.00		
Jelly Compote	175.00		150.00	200.00		
Nappy, Hndl., Rare				425.00		
Pitcher	450.00			475.00		
Tumbler	100.00			100.00		
Plate, 8", Rare	600.00			600.00		
Spooner	150.00			150.00		
Stemmed Card Tray, Rare	500.00			500.00		
Sugar	225.00			225.00		
Wine, V. Rare				425.00		
Panelled Flowers						
Nut Cup, Ftd.	85.00		50.00			
Rose Bowl, Ftd.	75.00		45.00			
Panelled Holly						
Bowl, Master	200.00		150.00			
Bowl, Sauce	75.00		35.00			
Butter	400.00		325.00			
Creamer	175.00		125.00			
Novelty Bowl	90.00		65.00			
Pitcher	850.00		600.00			
Tumbler	125.00		100.00			
Shakers, Pr.	275.00		175.00			
Spooner	175.00		125.00			
Sugar	275.00		200.00			
Panelled Sprig						
Cruet			150.00			
Shakers, Pr.			125.00			
Toothpick Holder			100.00			
Peacock Tail						
Tumbler, Rare	100.00	95.00	75.00			
Peacocks (On The Fence)						
Bowl, Scarce	300.00		165.00			375.00 Cobalt
Pearl Flowers						
Novelty Bowl, Ftd.	60.00	50.00	30.00			
Nut Bowl, Ftd.	50.00	45.00	35.00			
Rose Bowl, Ftd.	70.00	80.00	40.00			
Pearls & Scales						
Compote	65.00	60.00	40.00	75.00		80.00 Emerald
Rose Bowl, Rare	100.00	100.00	60.00	95.00		110.00 Emerald
Piasa Bird						
Bowl	55.00		45.00			
Plate, Ftd.	125.00		100.00			
Rose Bowl	90.00		75.00			
Spittoon Whimsey	95.00		85.00			
Vase	75.00		65.00			
Picadilly						
Basket, Sm.	100.00	90.00	70.00			
Picket						
Planter	75.00		60.00	75.00		

	Blue	Green	White	Vaseline/ Canary	Cranberry	Other
Pinecones & Leaves						
Bowl			70.00			
Pineapple & Fan						
Vase				400.00		
Plain Jane						
Nappy, Ftd.	50.00	60.00	30.00	85.00		
Plain Panels						
Vase	45.00	40.00	30.00			
Plume Panels Vt.						
Vase, V. Rare	250.00	250.00	150.00			
Poinsettia						
Fruit Bowl	125.00	110.00	85.00		175.00	
Pitcher, Either Shape	350.00 – 500.00	375.00 – 550.00	250.00 – 400.00		750.00 – 1,300.00	
Tumbler	75.00		45.00		125.00	
Sugar Shaker	300.00	300.00	200.00		450.00	
Syrup, Various	300.00 – 700.00	350.00 – 750.00	200.00 – 450.00		450.00 – 900.00	
Poinsettia Lattice (Lattice & Poinsettia)						
Bowl, Scarce	450.00		150.00	600.00		
Polka Dot*						
Bowl, Lg.	75.00		50.00		125.00	
Cruet	400.00		250.00		750.00	
Pitcher, Rare	250.00		150.00		850.00	
Tumbler	70.00		30.00		125.00	
Shakers, Pr.	100.00		60.00		300.00	
Sugar Shaker	200.00		150.00		300.00	
Syrup	250.00		125.00		725.00	
Toothpick Holder	425.00		300.00		525.00	
Popsicle Sticks						
Bowl, Ftd.	55.00	50.00	35.00			
Pressed Coinspot (#617 or Concave Cloumns)						
Card Tray	75.00	100.00	50.00	100.00		
Compote	65.00	75.00	45.00	75.00		
Primrose (Daffodils Vt.)						
Pitcher			900.00			
Princess Diana						
Biscuit Set (Jar & Plate, Complete)	100.00			110.00		
Butter	125.00			110.00		
Compote, Metal Base	150.00			135.00		
Compote, Lg.	90.00			110.00		
Creamer	55.00			50.00		
Novelty Bowl	50.00			45.00		
Open Sugar	70.00			65.00		
Pitcher	150.00			120.00		
Tumbler	50.00			40.00		
Plate, Crimped	65.00			60.00		
Salad Bowl	55.00			50.00		
Water Tray	55.00			50.00		
Prince William						
Creamer	65.00			60.00		
Open Sugar	65.00			60.00		
Oval Plate	50.00			50.00		
Pitcher	125.00			125.00		

	Blue	Green	White	Vaseline/ Canary	Cranberry	Other
Tumbler	45.00			35.00		
Toothpick Hldr.	65.00					
Pulled Loop						
Vase, 2 Sizes, Scarce	40.00 – 80.00	55.00 – 90.00	25.00 – 55.00			
Pump & Trough*						
Pump	130.00		100.00	125.00		
Trough	75.00		50.00	65.00		
Pussy Willow						
Vase, 4½"				70.00		
Queen's Crown						
Bowl, Sm.	40.00					
Compote, Low	60.00					
Queen's Spill						
Spill Vase, 4"	90.00			90.00		
Queen Victoria						
Plate, Ruffled	150.00			150.00		
Question Mark						
Card Tray	75.00					
Compote	70.00	85.00	45.00	150.00		
Quilted Daisy						
Fairy Lamp	500.00		375.00	450.00		
Quilted Pillow Sham						
Creamer	75.00			70.00		
Open Sugar	75.00			65.00		
Oval Butter	100.00			100.00		
Ray						
Vase	55.00	50.00	30.00			
Rayed Heart						
Compote	75.00	60.00	45.00			
Rayed Jane						
Nappy	50.00		25.00	65.00		
Reflecting Diamonds						
Bowl	60.00	65.00	40.00			
Reflections						
Bowl	50.00	50.00	30.00			
Regal (Northwood's)						
Bowl, Master	125.00	150.00	100.00			
Bowl, Sauce	35.00	45.00	20.00			
Butter	225.00	175.00	125.00			
Celery Vase	150.00	175.00	100.00			
Creamer	100.00	65.00	50.00			
Cruet	800.00	800.00	700.00			
Plate, Rare	165.00	150.00	100.00			
Pitcher	325.00	300.00	200.00			
Tumbler	100.00	85.00	45.00			
Shakers, Pr.	400.00	400.00	325.00			
Spooner	100.00	65.00	50.00			
Sugar	150.00	100.00	70.00			
Reverse Drapery						
Bowl	45.00	45.00	25.00			
Plate	90.00	85.00	50.00			
Vase	40.00	40.00	30.00			

	Blue	Green	White	Vaseline/ Canary	Cranberry	Other
Reverse Swirl						
Bowl, Master	70.00		40.00	55.00	85.00	
Bowl, Sauce	25.00		20.00	25.00	40.00	
Butter	200.00		165.00	175.00	250.00	
Celery Vase	175.00		100.00	150.00	200.00	
Creamer	125.00		100.00	125.00	195.00	
Cruet	275.00		110.00	175.00	475.00	
Cruet Set & Holder,						
4 Pcs.	300.00		200.00		375.00	
Custard Cup	50.00		35.00		150.00	
Finger Bowl	70.00		45.00		100.00	
Hanging Lamp, Rare					1,700.00	
Mini-Lamp	375.00		200.00		325.00	
Mustard Pot	80.00		45.00	75.00	125.00	
Oil Lamp	350.00		300.00	345.00		
Pitcher	250.00		175.00	225.00	800.00	
Tumbler	60.00		35.00	60.00	100.00	
Shakers, Pr.	100.00		60.00	100.00	175.00	
Spooner	125.00		80.00	100.00	150.00	
Sugar	175.00		100.00	150.00	225.00	
Sugar Shaker	175.00		125.00	150.00	275.00	
Syrup	175.00		100.00	150.00	425.00	
Toothpick Holder	155.00		100.00	125.00	275.00	
Water Bottle	150.00		100.00	150.00	200.00	
Rib & Big Thumbprints						
Vase	45.00	40.00	25.00			
Ribbed Coinspot						
Celery Vase, Rare					300.00	
Creamer, Rare					500.00	
Pitcher, Rare					1,100.00	
Tumbler, Rare					200.00	
Sugar Shaker					550.00	
Syrup, Rare					1,400.00	
Ribbed Lattice						
Bowl, Master	70.00		45.00		150.00	
Bowl, Sauce	30.00		20.00		40.00	
Butter	225.00		175.00		800.00	
Creamer	75.00		65.00		400.00	
Cruet	225.00		175.00		500.00	
Pitcher	275.00		225.00		1,000.00	
Tumbler	50.00		40.00		150.00	
Shakers, Pr.	145.00		100.00		300.00	
Spooner	75.00		65.00		400.00	
Sugar	125.00		100.00		650.00	
Sugar Shaker, 2 Sizes	140.00		100.00		425.00	
Syrup	175.00		150.00		600.00	
Toothpick Holder	300.00		175.00		350.00	
Ribbed Opal Rings						
Pitcher, Rare					825.00	
Tumbler					125.00	
Ribbed Optic						
Tumble-up	70.00	80.00	50.00	75.00	100.00	
Ribbed Spiral						
Bowl, Master	75.00		45.00	65.00		

	Blue	Green	White	Vaseline/ Canary	Cranberry	Other
Bowl, Sauce	30.00		20.00	25.00		
Bowl, Ruffled	55.00		40.00	50.00		
Butter	375.00		300.00	350.00		
Creamer	100.00		45.00	65.00		
Cup & Saucer	110.00		60.00	100.00		
Jelly Compote	70.00		50.00	65.00		
Pitcher	525.00		385.00	475.00		
Tumbler	115.00		60.00	100.00		
Plate	75.00		45.00	60.00		
Shakers, Pr.	225.00		125.00	225.00		
Spooner	110.00		50.00	75.00		
Sugar	200.00		150.00	175.00		
Toothpick Holder	175.00		125.00	175.00		
Vase, Squat, 4" – 7"	60.00		35.00	75.00		
Vase, Standard, 8" – 14"	45.00		25.00	55.00		
Vase, Funeral, 15" – 22"	145.00		90.00	200.00		
Whimsey, 3 Hndl.				125.00		
Richelieu						
Basket, Hndl.	100.00		60.00	80.00		
Bowl	70.00		50.00	65.00		
Cracker Jar w/lid	200.00		150.00	185.00		
Creamer	65.00		45.00	60.00		
Divided Dish, Rare	100.00		75.00	100.00		
Jelly Compote	75.00		50.00	75.00		
Nappy, Hndl.	90.00		70.00	95.00		
Open Sugar	65.00		40.00	60.00		
Basket, Open	100.00		70.00	100.00		
Pitcher	160.00		130.00	150.00		
Tumbler	30.00		20.00	30.00		
Tray	65.00		40.00	55.00		
Triple Sweet Dish	75.00		60.00	75.00		
Ric-Rac						
Jar				100.00		
Ring Handle						
Ring Tray	100.00	80.00	75.00	95.00		
Shakers, Pr.	100.00		75.00			
Ripple						
Vase	125.00	110.00	75.00	125.00		
Rippled Rib						
Vase			40.00			
Rococo						
Bowl, Bride's Basket	300.00		250.00	300.00	400.00	
Plate, 10", Rare	400.00		350.00	400.00	600.00	
Rose (also called Rose & Ruffles)						
Candlesticks, Pr.	250.00			250.00		
Cologne	250.00			250.00		
Vase, 6"	100.00			100.00		
Powder Jar, 2 Sizes	125.00			125.00		
Pomade	100.00			100.00		
Covered Bowl, Lg.	150.00			150.00		
Tray, Dresser	100.00			100.00		
Pin Tray or Soap Dish	75.00			75.00		
Tall Compote	100.00			100.00		

	Blue	Green	White	Vaseline/ Canary	Cranberry	Other
Console Bowl	80.00			80.00		
Tray, Cntr. Hndl.	90.00			90.00		
Rose Show						
Bowl, Rare	325.00		210.00			
Rose Spatter						
Pitcher, Rare						400.00 Tortoise Shell
Rose Spray						
Compote	50.00	60.00	30.00			85.00 Amethyst
Roulette						
Novelty Bowl	50.00	45.00	30.00			
Plate	100.00	100.00	60.00			
Royal Jubilee						
Basket, Hndl.	110.00			110.00		125.00 Amber
Royal Scandal						
Wall Vase	250.00		200.00	250.00		
Rubina Verde						
Vase					300.00	
Ruffles & Rings						
Novelty Bowl	55.00	50.00	30.00			
Nut Bowl	60.00	55.00	40.00			
Rose Bowl	65.00	60.00	45.00			
Ruffles & Rings w/Daisy Band						
Bowl, Ftd.	125.00	110.00	65.00			
S-Repeat						
Bowl, Master	85.00	100.00	65.00			
Pitcher	500.00		350.00			
Tumbler	65.00		45.00			
Scheherezade						
Novelty Bowl	50.00	45.00	30.00			
Scottish Moor						
Celery Vase	150.00		100.00			
Cracker Jar	350.00		225.00			
Cruet	400.00		225.00			
Fluted Vase	110.00		85.00			
Pitcher	350.00		275.00		475.00	400.00 Rubina
Tumbler	80.00		65.00		100.00	100.00 Amethyst
Scroll with Acanthus						
Bowl, Master	55.00		40.00	50.00		
Bowl, Sauce	25.00		20.00	25.00		
Butter	375.00		325.00	350.00		
Creamer	100.00		65.00	75.00		
Cruet	225.00		200.00	375.00		
Jelly Compote	65.00		60.00	65.00		
Pitcher	400.00		325.00	350.00		
Tumbler	100.00		65.00	75.00		
Shakers, Pr.	225.00		195.00	200.00		
Spooner	85.00		70.00	75.00		
Sugar	175.00		150.00	165.00		
Toothpick Holder	300.00		275.00	325.00		
Sea Scroll						
Compote	150.00	145.00	100.00			
Seafoam						
Compote	275.00		200.00			

	Blue	Green	White	Vaseline/ Canary	Cranberry	Other
Seaspray						
Nappy	45.00	45.00	35.00			
Whimsey	50.00	50.00	40.00			
Seaweed						
Bowl, Master	60.00		40.00		125.00	
Bowl, Sauce	30.00		20.00		70.00	
Butter	200.00		125.00		400.00	
Celery Vase	100.00		80.00		175.00	
Creamer	125.00		100.00		225.00	
Cruet, 2 Shapes	250.00		150.00		700.00	
Pitcher	350.00		250.00		450.00	
Tumbler	70.00		45.00		125.00	
Pickle Castor, Complete					650.00	
Rose Bowl			500.00			
Shakers, Pr.	150.00		125.00		350.00	
Spooner	125.00		100.00		175.00	
Sugar	175.00		145.00		225.00	
Sugar Shaker	225.00		175.00		425.00	
Syrup	175.00		150.00		535.00	
Toothpick Holder	325.00		225.00		500.00	
Serpent Threads						
Epergne, 23"				300.00		
Shell Beaded						
Bowl, Master	85.00	100.00	65.00			
Bowl, Sauce	55.00	65.00	35.00			
Butter	500.00	675.00	400.00			
Condiment Set, 4 Pcs.	800.00	900.00	700.00			
Creamer	150.00	180.00	145.00			
Cruet	500.00	700.00	400.00			
Pitcher	575.00	625.00	500.00			
Tumbler	100.00	115.00	75.00			
Shakers, Pr.	350.00	400.00	300.00			
Spooner	150.00	180.00	150.00			
Sugar	225.00	275.00	190.00			
Toothpick Holder	475.00	675.00	500.00			
Jelly Compote, V. Rare	900.00	900.00	700.00	900.00		
Shell & Dots						
Novelty Bowl	50.00		40.00	100.00		
Rose Bowl	45.00		35.00			
Nut Bowl	45.00	55.00	40.00			
Shell & Wild Rose						
Novelty Bowl, Open Edge	60.00	55.00	45.00	100.00		
Silver Overlay						
Vase			75.00			
Simple Simon						
Compote	65.00	60.00	40.00			
Singing Birds						
Mug, Rare	400.00		350.00	600.00		
Single Lily Spool						
Epergne	175.00	170.00	125.00	250.00		
Single Poinsettia						
Bowl			275.00			
Sir Lancelot						
Bowl, Ftd.	65.00	60.00	40.00			

	Blue	Green	White	Vaseline/ Canary	Cranberry	Other
Smooth Rib						
Bowl				35.00		
Snowflake						
Hand Lamp	400.00		275.00		600.00	
Night Lamp	1300.00		800.00		1,800.00	
Oil Lamp	325.00		225.00		550.00	
Somerset						
Oval Dish, 9"	45.00			35.00		
Pitcher, Juice, 5½"	60.00			50.00		
Tumbler, 3"	30.00			25.00		
Square Dish	50.00			45.00		
Sowerby Salt						
Salt Dish	65.00	70.00	55.00			
Spanish Lace*						
Bowl, Master	100.00		65.00	80.00	150.00	
Bowl, Sauce	30.00		25.00	30.00	40.00	
Bride's Basket, 2 Sizes	125.00		90.00	150.00	200.00	
Butter	425.00		225.00	400.00	500.00	
Celery Vase	125.00		85.00	150.00	175.00	
Cracker Jar	700.00				900.00	
Creamer	150.00		100.00	125.00	175.00	
Cruet	275.00		200.00	300.00	750.00	
Finger Bowl	75.00		50.00	85.00	150.00	
Jam Jar	300.00		200.00	325.00	500.00	
Liquor Jug					850.00	
Mini-Lamp	200.00		125.00	225.00	350.00	
Pitcher	250 – 500.00		100 – 300.00	225 – 450.00	650.00 – 1,000.00	
Tumbler	60.00		40.00	55.00	125.00	
Perfume Bottle	300.00		100.00	225.00	275.00	
Rose Bowl, Many Shapes	75.00		50.00	75.00	150.00	
Shakers, Pr.	125.00		75.00	125.00	225.00	
Spooner	150.00		100.00	145.00	175.00	
Sugar	275.00		200.00	250.00	325.00	
Sugar Shaker	150.00		100.00	150.00	225.00	
Syrup	250.00		175.00	350.00	650.00	
Vase, Many Sizes	100.00		50.00	125.00	225.00	
Water Bottle	300.00		200.00	325.00	425.00	
Spatter						
Vase, 9"	95.00	90.00	55.00	100.00		
Bowl	55.00	50.00	30.00	55.00	125.00	
Pitcher	250.00	250.00	175.00	265.00	450.00	
Tumbler	35.00	35.00	20.00	30.00	95.00	
Spattered Coinspot						
Pitcher					450.00	
Tumbler					100.00	
Speckled Stripe						
Barber Bottle	290.00		265.00	290.00		
Sugar				50.00		
Vase, 3 Sizes	110.00 – 200.00	100.00 – 190.00	75.00 – 150.00	100.00 – 185.00		
Shakers, Pr.	240.00		190.00	240.00		
Covered Jar	390.00		350.00	390.00		
Spokes & Wheels						
Bowl	55.00	50.00	35.00			
Plate, Rare	85.00	80.00				75.00 Aqua

	Blue	Green	White	Vaseline/ Canary	Cranberry	Other
Spool						
Compote	50.00	50.00	35.00			
Spool of Threads						
Compote	60.00		40.00	55.00		
Squirrel & Acorn						
Bowl	185.00	175.00	170.00			
Compote	190.00	180.00	175.00			
Vase	190.00	180.00	175.00			
Whimsey	190.00	185.00	175.00			
Stag & Holly						
Bowl, Ftd., Rare			1,500.00			2,000.00 Amethyst
Star Base						
Sq. Bowl	40.00					
Stars & Bars						
Pull Knob, Ea.			20.00			
Stars & Stripes						
Barber Bottle			100.00		300.00	
Compote (Age ?)					375.00	
Lamp Shade			65.00			
Pitcher			250.00		1,150.00	
Tumbler	100.00		75.00			
Stork & Rushes						
Mug	125.00		175.00			
Tumbler			65.00			
Stork & Swan						
Syrup			150.00			
Strawberry						
Bon-Bon			225.00			
Bowl						125.00 Amethyst
Stripe*						
Barber Bottle	160.00				300.00	
Bowl			60.00		100.00	
Condiment Set	400.00				750.00	
Cruet					500.00 – 750.00	
Oil Lamp					625.00	
Pitcher	275.00			350.00	575.00	
Tumbler	55.00			70.00	100.00	
Rose Bowl	100.00				225.00	
Shakers, Pr.	100.00				250.00	
Syrup	275.00				450.00	
Toothpick Holder	250.00				400.00	
Vase			600.00		125.00	
Stripe, Wide						
Cruet	200.00	500.00	175.00		550.00	
Pitcher	250.00		175.00		450.00	
Tumbler	60.00		40.00		100.00	
Shakers, Pr.			150.00		250.00	
Sugar Shaker	175.00		150.00		275.00	
Syrup	225.00		200.00		325.00	
Toothpick Holder	275.00	400.00	225.00		350.00	
Sunburst on Shield (Diadem)						
Bowl, Master	150.00			200.00		
Bowl, Sauce	40.00			40.00		
Breakfast Set, 2 Pcs.	200.00			250.00		

	Blue	Green	White	Vaseline/ Canary	Cranberry	Other
Butter	375.00		275.00	400.00		
Creamer	150.00		100.00	145.00		
Cruet, Rare	325.00		350.00	750.00		
Nappy, Rare	225.00			350.00		
Pitcher	600.00			950.00		
Tumbler	125.00			200.00		
Spooner	150.00		100.00	145.00		
Sugar	225.00		175.00	250.00		
Novelty Bowl, 7½"	100.00		75.00	100.00		
Sunk Hollyhock						
Bowl, Scarce				100.00		
Sunk Honeycomb						
Bowl, V. Rare				200.00		
Surf Spray						
Pickle Dish, V. Scarce	70.00	65.00	45.00			
Swag with Brackets						
Bowl	50.00	45.00	30.00	45.00		
Bowl, Master	78	65.00	45.00	65.00		
Bowl, Sauce	35.00	35.00	25.00	30.00		
Butter	275.00	250.00	200.00	250.00		
Creamer	100.00	85.00	55.00	80.00		
Cruet	500.00	325.00	175.00	250.00		
Jelly Compote	60.00	55.00	30.00	50.00		
Pitcher	300.00	300.00	200.00	290.00		
Tumbler	85.00	75.00	40.00	75.00		
Shakers, Pr.	200.00	175.00	125.00	200.00		
Spooner	100.00	110.00	55.00	100.00		
Sugar	150.00	140.00	75.00	125.00		
Toothpick Holder	350.00	300.00	250.00	300.00		
Whimsey Sugar	175.00			175.00		
Swastika						
Pitcher	900.00	900.00	675.00		1,100.00	
Tumbler	100.00	125.00	85.00		175.00	
Syrup	950.00	950.00	850.00		1,325.00	
Swirl						
Bowl, Master	50.00	55.00	40.00		75.00	
Bowl, Sauce	20.00	25.00	15.00		35.00	
Butter	125.00	125.00	65.00		175.00	
Cheese Dish			250.00		400.00	
Celery Vase	75.00	85.00	50.00		150.00	
Creamer	75.00	85.00	40.00		100.00	
Cruet, 2 Sizes	175.00	200.00	100.00		300.00	
Cruet Set, Complete					475.00	
Custard Cup	40.00	50.00	30.00		75.00	
Finger Bowl	65.00	60.00	35.00		100.00	
Fingerlamp			350.00		600.00	
Lampshade	100.00	100.00	40.00		175.00	
Mustard Jar	100.00	110.00	60.00		150.00	
Pitcher, Various	125.00 – 225.00	115.00 – 200.00	60.00 – 110.00	300.00	250.00 – 600.00	
Tumbler	30.00	25.00	15.00	45.00	95.00	
Rose Bowl	60.00	70.00	40.00		90.00	
Shakers, Pr.	175.00	150.00	100.00		250.00	
Shot Glass	80.00		65.00			
Spooner	75.00	80.00	40.00		125.00	

	Blue	Green	White	Vaseline/ Canary	Cranberry	Other
Strawholder, Rare	800.00		575.00		1,200.00	
Sugar	100.00	110.00	50.00		175.00	
Sugar Shaker	150.00	100.00	75.00		175.00	
Syrup	125.00	115.00	75.00		160.00	
Toothpick Holder	125.00	140.00	70.00		150.00	
Vase	60.00	65.00	35.00		150.00	
Water, Bitters & Bar						
Bottles, Ea.	100.00 – 250.00	90.00 – 200.00	65.00 – 100.00		350.00 – 450.00	
Swirling Maze						
Bowl, Salad	100.00	90.00	60.00		150.00	
Pitcher, any, (avg.)	500.00	450.00	300.00		800.00	
Tumbler	65.00	55.00	25.00		100.00	
Target						
Vase	125.00	85.00	65.00			
Thin & Wide Rib						
Vase	50.00	50.00	35.00	50.00		
Thistle Patch (Intaglio Poppy)						
Novelty, Ftd.	90.00		40.00	75.00		
Add 10% for Goofus						
Thorn Lily						
Epergne				300.00		
Thousand Eye						
Bottles, Various			25.00 – 55.00			
Bowls, Various			25.00 – 50.00			
Butter			125.00			
Celery Vase			100.00			
Compotes, Various			45.00 – 85.00			
Creamer			75.00			
Cruet			150.00			
Pitcher			110.00			
Tumbler			30.00			
Shakers, Pr.			75.00			
Spooner			75.00			
Sugar			100.00			
Toothpick Holder			125.00			
Thread & Rib						
Epergne	800.00	900.00	600.00	800.00		
Threaded Grape						
Compote, 8", Lg.	200.00	175.00	100.00			
Three Fingers & Panel						
Bowl, Master, Rare	100.00		75.00	100.00		
Bowl, Sauce, Rare	40.00		25.00	40.00		
Three Fruits						
Bowl, Scarce	225.00		145.00			
Three Fruits w/Meander						
Bowl, Ftd.	185.00		125.00			
Tines						
Vase		75.00				
Tiny Tears						
Vase	50.00	45.00	35.00			
Tokyo*						
Bowl, Master	45.00	40.00	25.00			
Bowl, Sauce	30.00	30.00	15.00			
Butter	200.00	175.00	100.00			

	Blue	Green	White	Vaseline/ Canary	Cranberry	Other
Creamer	100.00	80.00	40.00			
Cruet	200.00	200.00	100.00			
Jelly Compote	55.00	55.00	30.00			
Pitcher	350.00	300.00	175.00			
Tumbler	75.00	70.00	45.00			
Plate	70.00	70.00	35.00			
Shakers, Pr.	100.00	85.00	45.00			
Spooner	100.00	85.00	45.00			
Sugar	150.00	135.00	60.00			
Syrup	150.00	145.00	70.00			
Toothpick Holder	250.00	200.00	125.00			
Vase	55.00	50.00	35.00			
Trafalger Fountain						
Epergne	300.00		250.00	300.00		350.00 Amber
Trailing Vine						
Novelty Bowl	60.00		40.00	55.00		
Tree of Life						
Vase	100.00		60.00			
Shakers, ea.	100.00		50.00			
Tree of Love						
Butter, Covered, Rare			350.00			
Compote			55.00			
Novelty Bowl			45.00			
Plate, Rare, 2 Sizes			135.00			
Tree Stump						
Mug	100.00	110.00	65.00			
Tree Trunk						
Vase	45.00	50.00	35.00			
Trellis						
Tumbler				65.00		
Triangle						
Match-holder	75.00		55.00			
Trout						
Bowl			150.00			
Twig						
Vase, Sm., 5½"	65.00	75.00	50.00	75.00		
Vase, Panelled, 7"	85.00	100.00	65.00	85.00		
Vase Whimsey	100.00	110.00	80.00	75.00		
Twist (Miniatures)						
Butter	275.00		175.00	275.00		
Creamer	85.00		45.00	85.00		
Spooner	85.00		50.00	85.00		
Sugar	150.00		80.00	150.00		
Twisted Ribs						
Vase	45.00	40.00	25.00			
Twister						
Bowl	50.00	45.00	35.00			
Plate	100.00					
Vase Whimsey	75.00	75.00	45.00			
Venetian Beauty						
Lamp (Mini Night Lamp)	125.00		100.00		300.00	
Venetian (Spider Web)						
Vase	85.00					

	Blue	Green	White	Vaseline/ Canary	Cranberry	Other
Venice						
Oil Lamp	400.00		350.00			
Victoria & Albert						
Covered Butter	155.00		110.00	150.00		
Sugar	90.00		60.00	85.00		
Creamer	80.00		50.00	75.00		
Biscuit Jar	165.00		110.00	150.00		
Victorian						
Vase, applied flowers and vine	165.00	175.00	110.00	165.00		175.00 Amber
Victorian Hamper						
Handled Basket	75.00			75.00		
Vintage, Northwood/Dugan						
Bowl	55.00	55.00	30.00			
Plate	75.00	85.00	50.00			
Rose Bowl	65.00	65.00	35.00			
Vintage Leaf, Fenton						
Bowl, Rare	175.00					
Waffle						
Epergne						750.00 Olive
War of the Roses						
Bowl	75.00			70.00		
Boat Shape, Lg.	125.00			125.00		
Boat Shape, Sm.	100.00			100.00		
Compote, metal stand	150.00			150.00		
Waterlily & Cattails						
Bon-Bon	75.00	65.00	45.00			85.00 Amethyst
Bowl, Master	75.00	70.00	50.00			85.00 Amethyst
Bowl, Sauce	35.00	30.00	25.00			40.00 Amethyst
Breakfast Set, 2 Pcs.	150.00	135.00	100.00			175.00 Amethyst
Butter	400.00	350.00	250.00			425.00 Amethyst
Creamer	100.00	75.00	60.00			125.00 Amethyst
Gravy Boat, Hndl.	60.00	55.00	410.00			80.00 Amethsyt
Novelty Bowl	45.00	40.00	30.00			55.00 Amethyst
Pitcher	425.00	400.00	250.00			425.00 Amethyst
Tumbler	75.00	65.00	30.00			85.00 Amethyst
Plate	100.00	85.00	55.00			125.00 Amethsyt
Relish, Hndl.	100.00	90.00	70.00			125.00 Amethyst
Rose Bowl	85.00		50.00			135.00 Amethyst
Spooner	100.00	75.00	60.00			135.00 Amethyst
Sugar	200.00	150.00	100.00			225.00 Amethyst
Waterlily & Cattails (Northwood)						
Tumbler, Rare	100.00					
Wheel & Block						
Novelty Bowl	45.00	40.00	30.00			
Novelty Plate	135.00	100.00	65.00			
Vase Whimsey	55.00	45.00	35.00			
White Chapel						
Bowl	35.00			35.00		
Creamer	30.00			30.00		
Sugar, Open, Stemmed	35.00			35.00		
Wide Panel						
Epergne, 4 Lily, Scarce	800.00	850.00	600.00	925.00		

	Blue	Green	White	Vaseline/ Canary	Cranberry	Other
Wild Bouquet						
Bowl, Master	200.00	175.00	100.00			
Bowl, Sauce	65.00	50.00	40.00			
Butter	500.00	450.00	325.00			
Creamer	200.00	150.00	100.00			
Cruet	400.00	425.00	250.00			
Cruet Set w/tray	475.00	425.00	300.00			
Jelly Compote	175.00	135.00	100.00			
Pitcher	275.00	250.00	200.00			
Tumbler	120.00	100.00	50.00			
Shakers, Pr.	200.00	175.00	125.00			
Spooner	200.00	150.00	100.00			
Sugar	300.00	275.00	195.00			
Toothpick Holder	425.00	375.00	225.00			
Wild Daffodils						
Mug	85.00		65.00			100.00 Amethyst
Wild Grape						
Bowl			40.00			
Compote			40.00			
Wild Rose						
Banana Bowl	70.00		50.00			80.00 Amethyst
Bowl	60.00		40.00			75.00 Amethyst
William & Mary						
Butter, Covered	200.00			190.00		
Cake Plate, Stemmed	150.00			130.00		
Compote	100.00			90.00		
Creamer	65.00			60.00		
Master Salt	50.00					
Open Sugar, Stemmed	70.00			65.00		
Plate	100.00			95.00		
Wilted Flowers						
Bowl	50.00	60.00	40.00			
Handled Basket	100.00	110.00	65.00			
Windflower						
Bowl, Rare	175.00		125.00			
Nappy, Rare			300.00			
Windows (Plain)*						
Barber Bottle					325.00	
Fingerbowl	50.00		45.00		75.00	
Mini Lamp	175.00				1,850.00	
Oil Lamp					625.00	
Pitcher, Various	150.00 – 200.00		90.00 – 150.00		350.00 – 550.00	
Tumbler	55.00		35.00		125.00	
Shade	60.00		35.00		200.00	
Toothpick Holder					325.00	
Windows (Swirled)						
Barber Bottle	225.00		175.00		375.00	
Bowl, Master	55.00		40.00		100.00	
Bowl, Sauce	40.00		30.00		55.00	
Butter	400.00		300.00		550.00	
Celery Vase	100.00		50.00		175.00	
Creamer	100.00		75.00		225.00	
Cruet	325.00		225.00		475.00	
Cruet Set, Complete	275.00		200.00		625.00	

	Blue	Green	White	Vaseline/ Canary	Cranberry	Other
Mustard Jar	75.00		55.00		150.00	
Pitcher, Various	300.00 – 425.00		200.00 – 300.00		600.00 – 800.00	
Tumbler	85.00		65.00		125.00	
Plate, 2 Sizes	125.00		65.00		250.00	
Shakers, Pr.	175.00		125.00		300.00	
Spooner	10.00		75.00		225.00	
Sugar	250.00		175.00		350.00	
Sugar Shaker	150.00		125.00		325.00	
Syrup, 2 Shapes	300.00		200.00		500.00	
Toothpick Holder	300.00		175.00		375.00	
Windsor Stripe						
Vase					125.00	
Winged Scroll						
Nappy, Rare				150.00		
Winter Cabbage						
Bowl, Ftd.	50.00	45.00	35.00			
Winterlily						
Vase, Scarce	125.00	100.00	75.00			
Wishbone & Drapery						
Bowl	50.00	45.00	35.00			
Plate	60.00	60.00	50.00			
Wood Vine (Gaiety Base)						
Oil Lamp			450.00			
Woven Wonder						
Novelty Bowl	55.00		40.00			
Rose Bowl	60.00		45.00			
Wreath & Shell						
Bank Whimsey, Rare				235.00		
Bowl, Master	100.00		70.00	125.00		
Bowl, Sauce	40.00		25.00	35.00		
Butter	250.00		150.00	225.00		
Celery Vase	200.00		100.00	175.00		
Cracker Jar	600.00		475.00	550.00		
Creamer	175.00		85.00	150.00		
Ivy Ball, Rare	175.00		125.00	165.00		
Ladies Spittoon	100.00		65.00	125.00		500.00 Pink
Novelty Bowl	75.00	150.00	55.00	65.00		
Pitcher	600.00		200.00	375.00		
Tumbler, Flat or Ftd.	125.00		50.00	75.00		
Rose Bowl	100.00		65.00	85.00		
Salt Dip	140.00		85.00	100.00		
Spooner	175.00		80.00	125.00		
Sugar	200.00		100.00	150.00		
Toothpick Holder	300.00		200.00	275.00		
Note: Add 10% for Decorated Items.						
Wreathed Grape & Cable						
Orange Bowl, Ftd., V. Rare			350.00			
Zipper & Loops						
Vase, Ftd.	65.00	70.00	45.00